REFLECTIONS ON CONTEMPORARY
PSYCHOANALYTIC THOUGHT

REFLECTIONS ON CONTEMPORARY PSYCHOANALYTIC THOUGHT
The Lisbon Lectures

Edited by

Rui Aragão Oliveira
Maria José Gonçalves
João Seabra Diniz

PHOENIX
PUBLISHING HOUSE
firing the mind

First published in 2022 by
Phoenix Publishing House Ltd
62 Bucknell Road
Bicester
Oxfordshire OX26 2DS

British Library Cataloguing in Publication Data

A C.I.P. for this book is available from the British Library

ISBN-13: 978-1-800131-13-2

Typeset by Medlar Publishing Solutions Pvt Ltd, India

www.firingthemind.com

Contents

Part I: Psychoanalysis and contemporaneity

v

Part II: Theory of psychoanalytic technique

Acknowledgements

We would like to thank the *Revista Portuguesa de Psicanálise* for permission to use the following papers in this volume:

Chapter 2—Freud and culture, by Éric Smadja, *Revista Portuguesa de Psicanálise* (2015), *35*(2): 6–12.
Chapter 4—Virtual space, identity, and psychoanalysis: a new world or a dreadful voyage?, by Andrea Marzi, *Revista Portuguesa de Psicanálise* (2017), *37*(2): 7–14.
Chapter 8—Towards a two-track model for psychoanalysis, by Howard B. Levine, *Revista Portuguesa de Psicanálise* (2014), *34*(1): 7–12.

We are grateful to the *Psychoanalytic Psychotherapy* for permission to publish:

Chapter 9—Who is killing what or whom: some notes on the internal phenomenology of suicide, by David Bell, *Psychoanalytic Psychotherapy* (2001), *15*(1): 21–37.

The *American Journal of Psychoanalysis* has kindly granted permission to use the following paper:

Chapter 10—Achieving the elasticity of technique: Sándor Ferenczi's psychoanalytic project and journey, by Franco Borgogno, *American Journal of Psychoanalysis* (2001), *61*(4): 391–407.

About the editors and contributors

Editors

João Seabra Diniz is a full member and supervising analyst of the Portuguese Psychoanalytical Society (PPS) and International Psychoanalytical Association. He started his psychoanalytic training in Italy and continued it in Lisbon at PPS. For many years, he was involved in the formation of candidates for psychoanalysis. He is past president of the SPP and of the Institute of Psychoanalysis of Lisbon/PPS. He is the former director of the Social Action Service at Santa Casa da Misericórdia de Lisboa, and worked in the childhood and youth sector, where he collaborated in the launch of Adoption in Portugal. For some years, he collaborated with the Center for Judicial Studies, training in matters related to the abandonment and adoption of children. He is former national director of the Family and Child Support Project (PAFAC). He was a member of the National Commission for the International Year of the Child.

Maria José Gonçalves is a medical doctor, child psychiatrist, psychoanalyst, child psychoanalyst, and full member and supervising analyst of the Portuguese Psychoanalytical Society (PPS) and International Psychoanalytical Association (IPA). She is the former president of the PPS Board and Institute Board, and past director of the PPS Training Committee. In the PPS Institute, she promotes the training on psycho-analytic ethics. She was a former director of the Department of Child and Adolescent Psychiatry of the Pediatric Hospital in Lisbon, where she founded a mental health infancy unit. She has published numerous papers, especially on infant psychoanalysis and on clinical issues.

Rui Aragão Oliveira is a full member and supervising analyst of the Portuguese Psychoanalytical Society (PPS) and International Psycho-analytical Association. He is the director of the training committee of the PPS, past president of the PPS, past editor-in-chief of the *Portuguese Psychoanalytical Review*, and past editor of *Psychoanalysis Today*. He teaches at the Psychoanalytical Institute in Lisbon and has been working with clinical groups for the IPA with the three-level model. He has pub-lished on the theory of technique, paternal function, and clinical issues.

Contributors

David Bell is a past president of the British Psychoanalytical Society and has just retired from being consultant in charge of the Fitzjohns Unit, a service based in the adult department of the Tavistock, providing treat-ment for severe/complex disorder. He lectures and publishes on a wide range of subjects including the historical development of psychoanalytic concepts (Freud, Klein, and Bion), and the psychoanalytic understanding of severe disorder personalities. For his entire professional career he has been deeply involved in interdisciplinary studies—the relation between psychoanalysis and literature, philosophy, and socio-political theory. He has written numerous papers and chapters in books/monographs and edited four books: *Reason and Passion: A Celebration of the Works of Hanna Segal*; *Psychoanalysis and Culture: A Kleinian Perspective*; *Living on the Border: Psychotic Processes in the Individual, the Couple, and the Group*; *Turning the Tide: The Psychoanalytic Approach of the Fitzjohn's Unit to Patients with Complex Need*. He has also written one small book, *Paranoia*. He is one of the UK's leading psychiatric experts in asylum and immigration.

Franco Borgogno is a doctor in philosophy and psychology, and a training and supervising analyst of the Italian Psychoanalytical Society. Franco was scientific secretary/president of the Turin Centre of Psychoanalysis, and secretary of the Training Institute of Milan. He was full Professor of Clinical Psychology and founded the Doctorate School in Clinical and Interpersonal Relationships Psychology and the Specialization School in Clinical Psychology at Turin University. He has been chair of the Psychoanalysis and University Committee for the IPA; one of the founders of the International Sándor Ferenczi Foundation; and received the Mary Sigourney Award in 2010 and the Book Prize 2017 of the American Board and Academy of Psychoanalysis.

Luis J. Martín Cabré is a full member and training and supervising analyst of the Psychoanalytical Association of Madrid and the International Psychoanalytical Association; a training and supervising child and adolescent analyst; and a full member of the Italian Psychoanalytical Society. He is a member of the Spanish Society of Child and Adolescent Psychiatry and Psychotherapy; a member of the Psychosomatic Medicine Studies Institute (Madrid); a member of the International Association of the History of Psychoanalysis; founder member of the Sándor Ferenczi International Foundation; member of the European editorial board of *The International Journal of Psychoanalysis*, and of the *American Journal of Psychoanalysis*. He is past president of the Madrid Psychoanalytical Association and former European representative member of the board of the International Psychoanalytical Association (2015–2019).

R. D. Hinshelwood is a Fellow of the British Psychoanalytical Society, and a Fellow of the Royal College of Psychiatrists. He has worked for many years in the NHS in Britain, including a period as clinical director of the Cassel Hospital, and was subsequently Professor in the Centre for Psychoanalytic Studies in the University of Essex, where he is now Professor Emeritus. He has written widely on Kleinian psychoanalysis and has taken a special interest in the organisational dynamics of psychiatry and of psychoanalysis.

Howard B. Levine is a member of the American Psychoanalytic Association (APsaA), PINE, the Contemporary Freudian Society, and on the faculty of NYU Post-Doc's Contemporary Freudian Track. He is also on the editorial board of the *International Journal of Psychoanalysis* and *Psychoanalytic Inquiry*; editor-in-chief of the Routledge Wilfred Bion Studies Book Series; and in private practice in Brookline, Massachusetts. He is the author of *Transformations de l'Irreprésentable* (Ithaque, 2019) and the forthcoming *Affect, Representation and Language: Between the Silence and the Cry* (Routledge). His co-edited books include *Unrepresented States and the Construction of Meaning* (Karnac, 2013); *On Freud's Screen Memories* (Karnac, 2014); *The Wilfred Bion Tradition* (Karnac, 2016); *Bion in Brazil* (Karnac, 2017), and *André Green Revisited: Representation and the Work of the Negative* (Karnac, 2018).

Andrea Marzi, MD, is a psychiatrist and psychoanalyst, with a PhD in medical ethics, a full member of the International Psychoanalytical Association and of the Italian Psychoanalytical Society (Società Psicoanalitica Italiana), and active member of the American Psychoanalytic Association, holding in these fields several national and international functions in groups and committees. He has been Visiting Fellow at the University of Cambridge (UK), worked in the Department of Forensic Psychopathology, and he has been a former Professor of Developmental Psychology at the University of Siena. He is also supervisor in institutions and the NHS and was a member of the Committee for the review of the new edition of the Ethical Code of the Italian Psychoanalytical Society, and participated in the IPA Task Force on remote analysis in training. He has published several dozen scientific articles in national and international journals, and several books. The latest publications include: "Ciak si gira, psicoanalisi al cinema", about the relationship between cinema and psychoanalysis, and as author and editor, *Psicoanalisi, Identità and Internet* (*Psychoanalysis, Identity and the Internet*, Karnac, 2016), the first survey in Italian about virtual reality and psychoanalysis.

Sérgio Eduardo Nick is a medical doctor, psychiatrist, psychoanalyst, child and adolescent psychoanalyst (COCAP/IPA), as well as a postgraduate in child and adolescent psychiatry and psychotherapy by the Child Orientation Clinic from the Rio de Janeiro Federal University (UFRJ), and a post-graduate in child and adolescent law from the Rio de Janeiro University's Law School (UERJ). He is an effective member of the Brazilian Psychoanalytical Association of Rio de Janeiro/Rio II (SBPRJ) and a member of the International Psychoanalytical Association (IPA). He is co-author of several books and has been teaching at the SBPRJ's Institute, where he is a member of the directory board of the SBPRJ, as first secretary (2003–2004), vice-treasurer (1995–1996), and professional department director (2007–2008). He is a member of the directory board of FEBRAPSI, as publishing and publicising directory's secretary (2005–2007), as general secretary (2007–2009), and as superintendent (2009–2011). He is a member of the IPA's Congress Working Group for the Mexico City Congress (2011). He is former vice-president of the Brazilian Psychoanalytical Association of Rio de Janeiro/Rio II (2012–2014); former director of the Child and Adolescent Department at the Latin American Psychoanalytical Federation—FEPAL (2012–2014); past chair of the Scientific Programme Committee for the IPA Boston Congress (2015); and former vice-president of the International Psychoanalytical Association (2017–2021).

Leopold Nosek is a full member and training analyst of the Brazilian Society of Psychoanalysis of São Paulo (BSPSP) and the International Psychoanalytical Association (IPA). He was awarded the Sigourney Award/IPA in 2014. He is a physician at the Faculty of Medicine of the University of São Paulo, former assistant at the Instituto da Criança, Faculty of Medicine, University of São Paulo; and former director of the Therapeutic Community Enfance. He is past president of the Brazilian Society of Psychoanalysis of São Paulo (SBPSP); past president of the Brazilian Federation of Psychoanalysis (Febrapsi); past president of the Latin American Psychoanalytic Federation (FEPAL); former board member of the IPA; and the current chair of the IPA's think tank on the future of psychoanalysis committee. He is the editor of *Álbum de Família—Imagens Fontes e Ideias da Psicanálise em São Paulo* (Casa do Psicólogo) and author of *A Disposição para o Assombro* (Perspectiva). He is co-curator of the psychoanalysis and modernism exhibition at the Art Museum of São Paolo, Brazil; the Modern Art Museum in Rio de Janeiro; as well as Santander space in Porto Alegre, in 2000. Also in 2000, he was the organiser of the exhibition "Freud: Conflito e Cultura", Museum of Art of São Paulo and Museum of Modern Art

xvi   ABOUT THE EDITORS AND CONTRIBUTORS

of Rio de Janeiro (curated by the Library of the American Congress in Washington). In 2005, he was curator of the exhibition "Dor, Forma e Beleza", Estação Pinacoteca in São Paulo in association with Olívio Tavares de Araújo.

Fernando Orduz is a psychoanalyst, and a full member of the Colombian Psychoanalytic Society (SOCOLPSI) and the International Psychoanalytical Association (IPA). He is past president of SOCOLPSI (2012–2014) and former editor of the *Journal of Psychoanalysis* (SOCOLPSI) from 2008 to 2012. He is past president of FEPAL (Psychoanalytic Federation of Latin América) (2014–2016). He is also a psychologist with a master's degree in communication and culture; and a Professor for over thirty years at the Universidad Javeriana and Universidad del Norte. He is the former director of Fundaurbana (1998–2002). He has had three books published around urban culture and in 2000 he earned the literary creation award from the Instituto Distrital de Cultura y Turismo de Bogotá.

Éric Smadja is a psychiatrist, a psychoanalyst, a couples psychoanalyst, a member of the Société Psychoanalytique de Paris, a guest member of the British Psychoanalytical Society, and a member of the International Psychoanalytical Association (IPA). He works both in Paris and London. He is also an anthropologist, an associate member of the American Anthropological Association, and a member of the Society for Psychological Anthropology. In 2007, he was awarded the IPA's Prize for "Exceptional contribution made to psychoanalytical research". He is an international lecturer and his works are pluri- and interdisciplinary in nature. He is the author of several books, most recently, *On Symbolism and Symbolisation: The Work of Freud, Durkheim and Mauss* (Routledge, 2018).

Virginia Ungar, MD, is a training analyst at the Buenos Aires Psychoanalytic Association (APdeBA). She lives and practises in Buenos Aires, Argentina. She specialises in child and adolescent analysis, was the former Chair of the International Psychoanalytical Association's Child and Adolescent Psychoanalysis Committee (COCAP) and of the Committee for Integrated Training. She was given the Platinum Konex Award for Psychoanalysis in 2016. She was elected as president of the International Psychoanalytical Association in 2015, the first woman to hold that position since the institution's founding. She served in that position from 2017–2021.

Introduction

The past decade of the twenty-first century was a period of organisational restructuring inside the Portuguese Psychoanalytical Society, and an opportunity to define new lines for the future.

Thus, between 2010 and 2020, Lisbon received a considerable number of the International Psychoanalytical Association's outstanding psychoanalysts from all over the world. Always welcomed by the Portuguese Psychoanalytical Society, they presented their thoughts, reflections, and clinical investigations to a wide audience, essentially Portuguese psychoanalysts, but also to many mental health professionals, students, or other intellectuals.

We think that far beyond the simple exchange of experiences, these conferences, workshops, or working groups stimulated the psychoanalytic thinking, assuming a singular identity, expressed today with differentiated lines of work and a brilliant liveliness in Portugal.

We found it useful to bring together in one book some of the most significant works, historically contextualising the way they were received, the enthusiasm of their reception, and the transformations that they directly or indirectly promoted in the community of Portuguese psychoanalysts and many mental health professionals, students, or attentive and curious spirits of our culture.

In this sense, we did not limit ourselves to chronologically following the occurrence of events, but rather to group them in two large groups of lectures that took place in considerably different spaces and times, under the stimulating themes: "Psychoanalysis and contemporaneity"; and "Theory of psychoanalytic technique".

Rui Aragão Oliveira
Maria José Gonçalves
João Seabra Diniz

Part I

Psychoanalysis and contemporaneity

The institutional dynamics of psychoanalysis: the effect of the "development threatening idea"

R. D. Hinshelwood

Introduction by Maria José Gonçalves

Following the crisis that the Portuguese Psychoanalytical Society experienced between 2009 and 2010, several psychoanalysts, in conflict with the board, left the society and formed a new study group at the IPA. For their part, the non-dissident psychoanalysts felt the need to reflect on the movements that led to such a deep and hostile division within the group. They also wanted to understand how they could recover their thinking capacity in the face of the successive actings which had set in, as a reaction to what they considered to be an attack on their dignity.

It was in this context that in May 2011 we invited Robert Hinshelwood, a contributor to the field of research regarding the application of psychoanalytical thinking to the study of the dynamics of groups and organisations, to hold a conference at our society.

Robert Hinshelwood is a psychiatrist and psychoanalyst at the British Psychoanalytical Society, as well as a Professor at the University of Essex, Centre for Psychoanalytical Studies. Influenced by the thoughts of Klein and Bion, he developed forms of observation and understanding of groups in the light of the unconscious fantasies and anxieties of individuals which manifest themselves within organisations.

He has a vast editorial background which includes establishing journals as well as the publication of numerous articles and books, amongst which are *A Dictionary of Kleinian Thought* (1989), *Observing Organisations: Anxiety, Defence and Culture in Health Care* (2000), *Thinking about Institutions: Milieux and Madness* (2001), *Suffering Insanity: Psychoanalytic Essays on Psychosis* (2004).

At this conference, Hinshelwood, starting from the Bionian concepts of schism and development threatening ideas as defence mechanisms against "the pain of development", states that the divisions inside psychoanalytic societies constitute social defences against tensions at work. Citing "narcissism of minor differences" (Freud), he considers that countertransferential anxieties, particularly the uncertainty regarding the therapeutic efficacy of theoretical ideas, the pressure to alleviate the suffering of patients, the ambivalence of love/hate experienced in countertransference, find narcissistic comfort in belonging to a group organised theoretically and cohesively in the rejection of rivals.

Hinshelwood quotes Riccardo Steiner: "The militarisation of rival psychoanalytic groups (then) allows an inner conflict within the individual to be re-experienced as a conflict between groups."

As in the British Psychoanalytical Society, since the creation of the Portuguese Psychoanalytical Society, there have been two groups, Kleinians and Freudians, led by the two founders of the society, and in which the theoretical divergence between the groups maintained the balance necessary for the functioning of the society. When the ideological division which absorbed much of the tension inherent in group interactions faded away, individual conflicts of personal affirmation and power of some members surfaced, breaking the cohesion of the society.

To conclude, and as a way of diminishing the effect of these processes, the author recommends the inclusion of this theme in the training curricula of psychoanalytic societies, in the form of a study group for reflection on the unconscious phenomena of group dynamics.

* * *

I will start with a stern assessment:

> ... the militarization and polarisation of differences between groups and between members of groups themselves ... can lead to an endless paranoid "ping-pong" of accusations. Groups, even when composed of psycho-analysts, have inevitably unconscious, unresolved components ... Sometimes even psycho-analytic groups are defending themselves from primitive anxieties using primitive mechanisms of defence based on excessive idealisation and denigration. (Steiner, 1991, p. 918)

The International Psychoanalytical Association (IPA) was formed in 1911, and rapidly since then many national societies and institutes have been founded. This ensured the "movement" survived and flourished. Formed from the two groups in Vienna and Zurich, there was trouble from the beginning. There was strong rivalry over who organised conferences, and who took the most important official positions. This was so immediate it suggests hidden (in fact unconscious) dynamics (see Hinshelwood, 2018). Not only the IPA, but over more than a century, splitting and schisms within the member institutions have been more or less endemic. Psychoanalytic tribalism is our culture, or as some people suggest a religious fundamentalism:

> [B]asically a humanistic discipline has conceived and touted itself as a positivist science while organising itself institutionally as a religion ... It becomes problematic when analysts approach psychoanalysis with an inappropriate paradigm, "as if" it were a science or religion. (Kirsner, 2000, p. 233)

What is it about psychoanalysis which promotes religious war?

Trying to answer that question, we need to choose what terms to use: political (Kirsner, 2000); sociological (Rustin, 1991); or religious (Sorenson, 2000). However, we are of course at liberty to use a psychoanalytic framework for trying to understand this persisting phenomenon.

Although psychoanalysis is, in practice, a psychology of the individual it is *an interpersonal psychology of the individual*, as Freud claimed:

> In the individual's mental life someone else is invariably involved, as a model, as an object, as a helper, as an opponent: and so from the very first individual psychology, in this extended but entirely justifiable sense of the words, is at the same time social psychology as well. (Freud, 1921c, p. 69)

From *Totem and Taboo* (Freud, 1912–1913), his excursion into mythology with Jung (or maybe *against* Jung), Freud was promoting the understanding of society and social institutions in terms of psychoanalytic concepts. He contributed a series of notable contributions to this psychoanalytic sociology (Prager & Rustin, 1993), these were: *Group Psychology and the Analysis of the Ego* (Freud, 1921c); *Civilization and its Discontents* (Freud, 1930a); and *The Future of an Illusion* (Freud, 1927c). The importance of Freud's efforts is to supplement the other disciplines with the notion of the unconscious and its specific dynamics. We can, therefore, augment the approach to problems of psychoanalytic institutions with psychoanalytic ideas that have been evolved to uncover social and cultural issues that occur unconsciously between the members of our societies.

The British Psychoanalytical Society (BPaS)

It has often been admirably related that the BPaS has not suffered a schism of the kind that many others did. This is not strictly true, in fact it could be the reverse. The BPaS is also renowned for its controversial discussions centring around a series of meetings in 1943 to 1944 in which the Klein group were required to present and defend their innovative theories (King & Steiner, 1991). They did so with powerful intensity, and indeed with talent. In fact there was no overall winner between the Kleinians and the orthodox Freudians who had emigrated before the war from the Nazi persecution in Austria. It is well-known that the BPaS did not suffer a formal split as so many other societies around the world have. However there were extreme conditions at the time. In 1942, the BPaS was the only major psychoanalytic society left standing in Europe (apart from small societies in Switzerland and Sweden), and the US was in turmoil with its home-grown and unorthodox eclecticism and interpersonal brand of psychoanalysis being strongly attacked by the invading Austrian immigrants from Vienna (see Kirsner, 2000).

With psychoanalysis itself teetering on the brink there was probably extreme need to hold together, however much disagreement there was. More than that the psychoanalytic movement must have been seriously jolted by Freud's death in 1939, a reminder that nothing necessarily lasts.

The debates and group formations in the BPaS were attempting to deal with the contest between a commitment to innovation on one hand, and a reverential maintenance of the past on the other. The development of the Klein group was a venture, perhaps reckless, to push forward regardless of the rest of the Society. For instance, in a letter to Ernest Jones in 1941, Melanie Klein reflects on the problems of presenting her work to the rest of the Society:

> I am not despairing and if I have fifteen or twenty more years left to work I should be able to accomplish my task. But I realise how difficult it is and what powers of presentation would be needed to give evidence for the truth and importance of these findings. (quoted in Grosskurth, 1986, p. 283)

On the other hand, Anna Freud's work looked back in a persisting dedication to the work of her father. Young-Bruehl is explicit about this:

> Her labour of checking and revising all her father's maps of psychic life was not original in the sense that it revealed a mapless territory. But it provided her with a survey-making or synthetic sense that was without equal in her generation. (Young-Bruehl, 1988, p. 461)

One is clearly looking forward to original new work, and the other is looking back for consolidation not originality, so they were never going in the same direction.

Melanie Klein and Anna Freud were clearly very different people. And thus their relationships with psychoanalysis, and equally their relationships with children, with being a child (daughter) and with child analysis, were also very different. Following from these differences they developed different forms of analysis and different conclusions about child development. However, within their group context they came to represent a deep schism. Perhaps, partly on the basis of their striking character differences they become polarised into opposites.

In fact, their differences may have been previously exploited by Ernest Jones and Sigmund Freud to carry *their* own rivalry. The dissent by the British from the Viennese conformity had been controlled by the enduring loyalty that Jones and Freud had for each other. At the same time the quarrel between these two women seems to express some undercurrent, too. Jones was from a Welsh nonconformist background (religious protestant). He lived out a rivalry, one that was intermingled with his extreme loyalty to Freud. We might consider therefore that, by displacing one side of his relationship, his nonconformist rivalry onto a quarrel between their respective protégés, Jones could maintain his customary tactful adulation of Freud, so that their friendship and cooperation could continue unharmed. The complementary uncomplicated rivalry between Anna Freud and Melanie Klein allowed Jones and Freud an uncomplicated loyalty.

So, professional debate linked up with personal rivalries and formed a hostile *group* dynamic.[1] In particular, during the lead-up to the controversial discussions in 1943, a to-and-fro process of mutual influence went on between Anna Freud's group and Melanie Klein's: the scientific committee had asked for a Kleinian paper on "The role of introjection and projection of objects in the early years of development" to start the discussion off on internalisation and internal objects. This is in the context of the mystique that seemed to exist about a concept so elusive as the "internal object" (Hinshelwood, 1997). This had been a matter of considerable interest and also incomprehension throughout the 1930s. However, Susan Isaacs first paper moved the debate to an adjacent area. Her paper was on "The nature and function of phantasy" (Isaacs, 1948). Isaacs developed the points Melanie Klein had made about unconscious phantasy in a response when Anna Freud gave a paper

---

[1] In this connection it is worth noting the doctoral thesis of Simona Reghintovschi which sought a more formal research result on the inter-school aggression within psychoanalysis. She noted the "sibling" rivalry between analysands of the same training analyst, raising the question whether there is enough awareness and work in training analysis about this "sibling" configuration in the unconscious transference (and maybe countertransference).

on sublimation to the Society in 1939. It would appear that the "subli-mation debate" with Anna Freud had influenced the Kleinians. From this, the importance of the notion of phantasy must have emerged as a basic concept underlying the "internal object". They had been only half appreciated previously, so the Kleinians attempted to clarify further and, as it were, "prove" their own point about unconscious phantasy. The conceptual details became territory for hand-to-hand fighting. It concerned the necessity for addressing the here-and-now, because we cannot change history. The influence of unconscious phantasy is active all the time, and not just when, under stress, regression to a fixation point occurs. So, the total situation of the analytic session is a transfer-ence experience.

Thus, between 1939 and 1943 the Kleinians had driven Anna Freud back to her classical work on fantasy, but she in turn had driven the Klein group beyond internal objects and towards more fundamental work on unconscious phantasy. We can see not just the linear search for a greater and greater approximation to a truth. Instead, the development of each group's set of ideas and values was influenced, and pushed away, by the other. Mutual influencing of conceptual development came out of pressures from group dynamics and group identity, and it promoted greater and greater divergence.

The dynamic I am suggesting is that conflicts within individuals, an intrapsychic conflict, may be experienced instead as one between differ-ent groups, an intergroup conflict. It is comparable to Jaques' description:

> Individuals may put their internal conflicts into persons in the
> external world, unconsciously follow the course of the conflict by
> means of projective identification, and re-internalize the course
> and outcome of the externally perceived conflict by means of
> introjective identification. (Jaques, 1955, pp. 496–497)

Thus, the separation of the two groups was dialectically dependent on each other, their difference negotiated and exaggerated between them.

Personal stress and public defence

In this way differences of character may have emerged into intensely felt opposites between practising schools of psychoanalysts within the

BPaS. But this is not the whole story since divergent groups within psychoanalytic institutes do *not* all have this specific constellation of conditions that applied to the BPaS in the 1930s and 1940s. When personal issues are depersonalised to become a group phenomenon—in this case a schism, as we will call it—makes us suspicious that a defensiveness is operating at the level of the group and organisation.

Menzies (1960) described how the common stresses can greatly influence and distort the work we do and the way we do it. She researched the nursing service of a general hospital and how an unconscious defensiveness was expressed institutionally as specific work practices of a maladaptive kind that hindered the task of the nursing service as a whole. Ordinary mature individuals can come to function in a setting in which they are induced to operate with a level of defensive splitting which is far below their level of personal maturity. Ken Eisold (1994) has specifically discussed how a similar organisational defensiveness against a work anxiety may operate within psychoanalytic institutions:

> this social defence of intolerance ... has to do with the nature of analytic work: the anxieties analysts encounter in the course of their work that lead them to feel the need to know with certainty what they believe. (Eisold, 1994, p. 787)

Eisold argued in line with Bion's view, that schisms within psychoanalytic organisations are social defences protecting against the tensions in the work. So, anxieties in common in the work can form coordinated defences which manifest as institutional schism.

A factor common to many schismatic Institutes—in Paris, in London, in so many cities in the United States—is the stress of the work requiring considerable emotional effort by each practitioner for long periods of the day. In effect, the countertransference. Is there a sense that uncertainty arising from countertransference on our professional practice creates a stress, as Eisold argued, and it emerges as institutional schism within the psychoanalytic institution? Thus, in some way the group dynamic emerges as the schismatic problem of the institution that hides and protects the practitioner from his/her anxiety and uncertainty.

Schism and the development threatening idea

The BPaS presented a lively picture of a schism that contrasted a thirst for innovation with a stabilising focus on the original groundwork. Such a controversy over what constitutes the *real* psychoanalysis was never resolved. In 1921, Freud postulated what he called "the narcissism of minor differences" (Freud, 1930a) to describe how groups that are close to each other are the most aggravated by each other. This dynamic is reflected in the quote from Jaques above.

We can also turn to Bion's description of a group schism:

> The defence that schism affords against the development-threatening idea can be seen in the operation of the schismatic groups, ostensibly opposed but in fact promoting the same end. One group adheres to the dependent group … popularises established ideas by denuding them … The reciprocal group, supposedly supporting the new idea, becomes so exacting in its demands that it ceases to recruit itself. Thus both groups avoid the painful bringing together of the primitive and sophisticated that is the essence of the developmental conflict. (Bion, 1961, p. 159)

This was published in Bion (1952, p. 235) and might be a cryptic reference to the controversial discussions.

Though Bion's early group work is not completely psychoanalytic, he moved to a much more psychoanalytic approach after he qualified as a psychoanalyst in 1950. He began to use the notion of defence (as in the above passage) as a motivating force. Bion's hunch was that schism protects against the pain of development, and how could that be interconnected with the countertransference? Bion was not specific, but in this instance I shall suggest that, in this case, it is the development towards being able to tolerate uncertainty.

Uncertainty

If it is the case that a development-threatening idea presses itself upon analysts, then an institutional response can protect the members in the way that the culture of medical institutions protects nurses. Then maybe we can get a clue as to what the threatening idea is from the character of the institutional response. The characteristic responses are the fervent debates over conceptual correctness, and so I would suggest that schisms invariably take the form of intransigent attitudes towards theories.

Ideas have an important place in psychoanalytic work. Interpretations given to patients on the basis of their free associations always depend on general theories applied to particular cases. Psychoanalysts *need* ideas in order to work. They need the best ideas to work best, and to give their human patients the best chance. Not only do they need them to maximise their careers, but they need them to provide the best reparative care for those suffering patients. Although one can turn to the notion of a professional superego acquired through a long training, I suggest an added factor. It is the stress of working with those suffering people. There is a lot to say about such intimate contact with suffering others (Hinshelwood, 2004). There is something about our response to others who suffer. It engages an almost instinctual reaction. In the Kleinian framework, reparation has to undo the work of primitive omnipotent destructiveness—and hence are we in the realm of supernatural harm and cure? Someone who falls over in the street immediately gathers a small crowd, and an accident on the motorway ensures people slow down to look and create a traffic jam, even on the opposite carriageway. Our ideas have to be the best for the job, otherwise failure involves serious disappointment for *both* parties. The sufferer continues to suffer, but the helper fails to be a helper and becomes a sufferer too. And as Ricardo Steiner said above (1991, p. 918), even groups of psychoanalysts can use the primitive methods of defence.

Further, part of the countertransference, which is not often mentioned, is the way the psychoanalyst picks up the patient's pressing demand (Hinshelwood, 2016). Frequently, patients expect an unrealistic *omnipotent* care and cure. The patient arrives for a treatment with anxious hopes. He has suffered from his experiences which have not remitted under his own regime of self-care, over many years. He has been defeated, and cure seems absolutely beyond any expectation of anyone. What is impossible for him, he imagines, may well be impossible for anyone else. So, it may be natural to demand someone with quite omnipotent ability. That demand may often be difficult for the psychoanalyst to resist unconsciously, and he plays into the omnipotent wishful phantasy because it may match his own hopes of himself, for narcissistic or other reasons. So, a lot hangs on having the best ideas.

In non-psychoanalytic work, this attempt to meet a demand on this scale leads to "burnout". In psychoanalytic work, I hypothesise it leads to other symptoms, in particular the paranoid suspicion and grandiosity towards other schools of psychoanalysis that creates our group dynamics. We get obsessively focused on who has the right ideas, the best ideas.

There are many claims as to which are the best psychoanalytic ideas. Despite the fairness of the fine democratic principle of pluralism, it does not define the best. Indeed quite the opposite: it provides a supermarket aisle of alternatives. Democratically, the more freedom for new ideas, the more choice, but in practise the greater the choice the more uncertainty about which is best.

Britton and Steiner (1994) noted the phenomenon of overvaluing of ideas: "an overvalued idea is more likely to be sought when uncertainty cannot adequately be contained" (Britton & Steiner, 1994, p. 1070).

Uncertainty is especially persecuting for a psychoanalyst, and the relief of certainty can be sought by clutching at an interpretation which has arrived in his mind with little reality. Pressures in the analytic session lead him to foreclose, abolish his thinking, sever him from the reality of his patient, and attach him to a body of ideas comprising his psychoanalytic school. This is a kind of ideology that leads to a pseudo-certainty, so that meaning can be forced onto clinical material, rather as an ideologue compresses new data into his preconceived ideas. Britton and Steiner contrasted the overvaluing of an idea, for this purpose with a "selected fact" which Poincaré described thus:

> If a new result is to have any value, it must unite elements long since known, but till then scattered and seemingly foreign to each other, and suddenly introduce order where the appearance of disorder reigned. Then it enables us to see at a glance each of these elements in the place it occupies in the whole. Not only is the new fact valuable on its own account, but it alone gives a value to the old facts it unites. (Poincaré, 1914, p. 30)

The intuitive emergence of an idea brings together disparate facts into an ordered theory. As Bion added it needs a particular state of mind—reverie—to allow that emergence of a "sudden precipitating intuition" (Bion, 1967, p. 127), and not interrupt it by forcing meaning onto the material. At this point Bion's recommendation to abandon memory and desire comes to mind.

For the various reasons argued here, a psychoanalyst seeks the elusive comfort of certainty. A practitioner may gain it by jumping at an interpretation that embodies an idea he especially values. But that grasping and overvaluing can be institutionalised within a group to provide a collective comfort for all in the group.

On the basis of this formulation we can say that the idea that threatens the psychoanalyst is uncertainty. And we can see why. The problem is that without the tolerance of uncertainty there is no serious development. Each group clings to its own certainties, and rejects the threatening process of questioning and testing the ideas.

Instead we enter schisms. The capacity in groups to make either over- or under-valuations is enhanced; so is the capacity to believe intensely in those distorted evaluations, "the narcissism of minor differences" (Freud, 1930a, p. 114). One could say groups are narcissistic, but it is more that a group brings out and supports the narcissism of the individuals who make up the group. So, groups give a certainty to the individuals' belief that "we" are right and good, and at the same time, that "they" are wrong and bad. The narcissism is needed for a purpose of knowing we do right by our patients.

As Riccardo Steiner said, even psychoanalysts may defend "themselves from primitive anxieties using primitive mechanisms of defence based on excessive idealisation and denigration" (Steiner, 1991, p. 918). And that applies to idealising ideas.

Hate and ambivalence

Finally, why do psychoanalysts find themselves so *uncertain* in their work? Why do we doubt the benevolence of psychoanalytic care?

The answer, I suggest, is that our benevolence is sometimes spoiled. We love and care and cherish those who suffer, but not always. In other words there is a problem of hate in the countertransference, which mingles with the primitive need to care. As Winnicott said about mother's love which is real and powerful, but at the same time: "The mother, however, hates her infant from the word go" (Winnicott, 1949, p. 73), and he elaborated eighteen reasons why she hates her baby. "A mother", he goes on, "has to be able to tolerate hating her baby without doing anything about it" (p. 74). He conveys this is true of the analyst, who "must find himself in a position comparable to that of a mother of a newborn baby" (p. 74).

Even Freud, with his attempt at a scientific neutrality, confessed about psychotic patients:

> I did not like those patients … They make me angry and I find myself irritated to experience them so distant from myself and from all that is human. This is an astonishing intolerance which brands me a poor psychiatrist. (Freud, quoted in Dupont, 1988, p. 251)

And this is echoed by a stark comment from the writer Samuel Beckett, at a time when he was in therapy at the Tavistock Clinic with Bion: "[H]e was like a hunk of meat. There was no-one there. He was absent" (Beckett, quoted in Knowlson, 1996, p. 209).

Not all patients are lovable, or bring out the requisite response of care. In fact, probably no patient does so all of the time. Realistic ambivalence would be the more appropriate state of mind for the psychoanalyst. But I suggest that psychoanalytic trainings do not focus on that. All new psychoanalysts are therefore confronted with a specific development-threatening idea. That idea which threatens is the ambivalence of love *and* hate which can coexist in the feelings towards those that suffer. Is the real uncertainty at an unconscious level? Both love and hate can develop when we should be simply and only caring. The militarisation of rival psychoanalytic groups then allows an inner conflict within the individual to be re-experienced as a conflict between groups.

Conclusions

Central to this discussion is the role of intergroup processes to take on the intrapsychic conflict of the individuals. An individual is relieved by being able to simplify, even simplistically, and take only one side of the conflict by identifying with *his* group. In the world of inter-tribal psychoanalytic conflicts, the Klein group, for instance, serves some function for many other schools as representing the harshness towards patients which in fact we all feel at times. Narcissism of minor differences is a relief for us, the individuals, but lethal for psychoanalysis as a movement and as a profession.

Can psychoanalysts become more aware of this set of evasive group dynamics? Proposals that all psychoanalytic training should now include a period in a form of study group, could point to some recognition of our us-and-them dynamics. The importance of such a recommendation would rest on the ability of any such group study to recognise how vulnerable we (our narcissistic selves) are to our uncertainties in the face of our patient's omnipotent hopes, and how we project that doubt into other schools we identify as dubious and malign.

References

Bion, W. R. (1952). Group dynamics: a review. *International Journal of Psychoanalysis, 33*(2): 235–247.

Bion, W. R. (1961). *Experiences in Groups and Other Papers*. London: Tavistock.

Bion, W. R. (1967). Commentary. In: *Second Thoughts: Selected Papers on Psycho-Analysis*. London: Heinemann.

Britton, R., & Steiner, J. (1994). Interpretation: selected fact or overvalued idea? *International Journal of Psychoanalysis, 75*: 1069–1078.

Dupont, J. (1988). Ferenczi's "madness". *Contemporary Psychoanalysis, 24*(2): 250–261.

Eisold, K. (1994). The intolerance of diversity in psychoanalytic institutes. *International Journal of Psychoanalysis, 75*(4): 785–800.

Freud, S. (1912–1913). *Totem and Taboo. S. E., 13*: vii–162. London: Hogarth.

Freud, S. (1921c). *Group Psychology and the Analysis of the Ego. S. E., 18*: 65–144. London: Hogarth.

Freud, S. (1927c). *The Future of an Illusion. S. E., 21*: 1–56. London: Hogarth.

Freud, S. (1930a). *Civilization and its Discontents. S. E., 21*: 57–146. London: Hogarth.

Grosskurth, P. (1986). *Melanie Klein: Her World and her Work*. London: Hodder and Stoughton.

Hinshelwood, R. D. (1997). The elusive concept of "internal objects" (1934–1943). Its role in the formation of the Klein Group. *International Journal of Psychoanalysis, 78*(5): 877–897.

Hinshelwood, R. D. (2004). *Suffering Insanity: Psychoanalytic Essays on Psychosis*. London: Routledge.

Hinshelwood, R. D. (2016). *Countertransference and Alive Moments: Help or Hindrance*. London: Process Press.

Hinshelwood, R. D. (2018). Freud and/or Jung: a group dynamic approach. In: R. S. Brown (Ed.), *Re-Encountering Jung: Analytical Psychology and Contemporary Psychoanalysis* (pp. 20–30). London: Routledge.

Isaacs, S. (1948). The nature and function of phantasy. *International Journal of Psychoanalysis, 29*: 73–97.

Jaques, E. (1955). Social systems as a defence against persecutory and depressive anxiety. In: M. Klein, P. Heimann, & R. E. Money-Kyrle (Eds.), *New Directions in Psychoanalysis: The Significance of Infant Conflict in the Pattern of Adult Behaviour* (pp. 478–498). London: Karnac.

King, P., & Steiner, R. (Eds.) (1991). *The Freud–Klein Controversies 1941–1945*. London: Routledge.

Kirsner, D. (2000). *Unfree Associations: Inside Psychoanalytic Institutes*. London: Process Press.

Knowlson, J. (1996). *Damned to Fame: The Life of Samuel Beckett*. London: Bloomsbury.

Menzies, I. E. P. (1960). A case-study in the functioning of social systems as a defence against anxiety: a report on a study of the nursing service of a general hospital. *Human Relations, 13*(2): 95–121.

Poincaré, H. (1914). *Science and Method*. London: Thomas Nelson and Sons.

Prager, J., & Rustin, M. (Eds.) (1993). *Psychoanalytic Sociology*. London: Hodder Arnold.

Rustin, M. (1991). *The Good Society and the Inner World*. London: Verso.

Sorenson, R. L. (2000). Psychoanalytic institutes as religious denominations: fundamentalism, progeny, and ongoing reformation. *Psychoanalytic Dialogues, 10*(6): 847–874.

Steiner, R. (1991). Editorial comments. In: P. King & R. Steiner (Eds.), *The Freud–Klein Controversies 1941–1945* (pp. 914–919). London: Routledge.

Young-Bruehl, E. (1988). *Anna Freud: A Biography*. London: W. W. Norton.

Winnicott, D. W. (1949). Hate in the counter-transference. *International Journal of Psychoanalysis, 30*: 69–74.

CHAPTER 2

Freud and culture

Éric Smadja

Introduction by Maria José Gonçalves

Éric Smadja, a psychoanalyst and a member of the Société Psychana-
lytique de Paris as well as the International Psychoanalytical Association, is also a psychiatrist and anthropologist, and a member of
the American Anthropological Association and the Society for Psychological Anthropology. With numerous published books, he has
devoted his multidisciplinary research work to the study of the links
between psychoanalytic culture and the contemporary contributions
of anthropology and sociology.

   Éric Smadja has visited Lisbon several times, where he has forged
friendships within the Portuguese psychoanalytic community. He has
also had the opportunity to present and debate his ideas on Freudian culture and thought, at a time when the Portuguese Psychoanalytic Society had, as one of its main objectives, opened itself to the
non-psychoanalytic scientific and cultural community. Furthermore,
the interest in the articulation of psychoanalysis with other forms of
knowledge was a structuring vector of its functioning.

In this chapter, which the Portuguese journal *Revista Portuguesa de Psicanálise* published in 2015 and whose title refers to his 2013 book *Freud et la Culture*, Smadja proposes a critical reflection on the evolution of the concept of culture in Freud's work and distinguishes the nature of sociocultural productions as an object of psychoanalytical study, from the nature of social phenomena, defined and studied by disciplines such as sociology and anthropology, with their specific methodologies.

Smadja analyses the way Freud approaches social and cultural phenomena from the knowledge of individual psychic phenomena, on the assumption that the unconscious and its laws are common to all individuals and that there is an archaic heritage that passes from generation to generation. The original phantasies (seduction, castration, primitive scene) exist in the unconscious of all humans, whether they live in primitive or developed societies, giving rise to a common anthropological structure. This approach of the collective opposes the systemic perspective of the interdependence of social phenomena, without interference from the individual, defended by sociologists.

For Freud there is an interdependence between internal and external reality. The social context in which the individual exists influences the individual's psychic functioning, which in turn will influence the external reality, in a work "promoting a cultural superego which expresses itself through an ethic which regulates social relations" (*Kulturarbeit*).

I would add that it is this work of culture which makes the psychoanalytic movement crucial for an ethical and developed community, and it is the responsibility of the psychoanalysts to keep it alive.

* * *

Epistemological and methodological considerations

On several occasions, as his work progressed, Freud declared that psychoanalysis was a "bridge", a "link", or rather promised to be so, and in being so acquired a mediating function between the medical sciences, psychopathology, and the sciences of the mind, sciences of culture. Its very "essence" would consist in this bidirectional deployment. Indeed, as early as *The Interpretation of Dreams* (1900a) on, he maintained that the psychic processes at work in dream work are just as active in the production of symptoms as in producing cultural and social phenomena. Consequently, psychoanalysis is not reducible to psychopathology, but it also has things to say about normal psychic functioning and beyond that, about sociocultural creations.

Whence the "twofold epistemological connection" to which Paul-Laurent Assoun (1993) refers, which would confer a certain *legitimacy* upon its practice in the sociocultural field.

Of course, but upon what does he base this assertion?

Freud considers that one may assume that the most general facts of unconscious psychic life discovered by psychoanalysis—such as infantile sexuality, drive conflicts, fantasies, the Oedipus complex, forms of repression, and substitutive satisfactions, in particular—are present everywhere, may therefore also be found in the "most varied domains of human mental activity", among which he mentioned the existence of "many surprising analogies".

It is this very notion of "human mental activity"—that of communities and peoples, the unconscious processes and formations of which present analogies with individual psychic life—which authorises and legitimises Freud's transition from individual psychology to mass psychology, within a perspective, however, common to that developed by Wilhelm Wundt in his *Elemente de Völkerpsychologie* (1912). However, their treatment of the analogies would prove to be quite different from one another.

Thus, the field of symbolism, for example, common to every individual—normal, dreaming, and neurotic—and to every culture, enables Freud to situate psychoanalysis, its main concepts, and its techniques of investigation, in a central position midway between psychopathology and the cultural sciences. Through the symbolical, the connections are established between individual and collective human realities. It would be the same for religion, the object of analogies with neurotic and psychotic individual formations.

In so doing, Freud was not to recognise the distinctive, singular aspects of this sociocultural reality, either in its modes of functioning or in its productions, which differentiate it radically from individual psychic reality. He would create confusion between *the nature of the object* of his psychology of the masses or of peoples and that of the two disciplines contemporary with psychoanalysis: sociology and anthropology.

As a consequence, his methodology would principally consist in a *sudden, direct, massive transfer* of notions and concepts stemming from individual psychology—that of dreams and neuroses—to the field of psychology of the masses, therefore, actually to the vast domain encompassing society, culture, civilisation, community, and the masses, something which specialists in the social sciences would, as a whole, reproach him for.

Nevertheless, Freud was conscious of the risks and difficulties of this methodology, which he expressed in *Moses and Monotheism: Three Essays* (1939a) in particular, as well as considering it useless to conceive of the existence of a collective unconscious for these masses or peoples, in view of the fact that he considered that "the content of the unconscious is generally collective, the universal property of human beings".

It seems to me that, associated with this, is the statement that individual psychology is "also, right from the beginning, simultaneously" a form of social psychology owing to the significance accorded to the role played by the Other person throughout the subject's life. Freud designated these relations, entertained with this Other person, as being "social phenomena", hence an additional confusion in Freudian language with the terminology used by sociologists and anthropologists.

I would also like to bring up Freud's need to fairly regularly connect ontogenesis and phylogenesis, the childhood of the individual and the prehistory of peoples or the human race, in order to explore and make intelligible both the individual psyche and the psyche of the masses.

Furthermore, it seems important to me to recall one of the reasons Freud was interested in this field of the sciences of culture, which was *that of helping it to eliminate the quality of "strangeness" of individual formations, those of neurotic symptoms or dreams, therefore of confirming the validity of the findings of psychoanalysis.* Indeed, in his *Introductory Lectures on Psycho-Analysis* (1916–1917), in particular, he spoke of the work of psychoanalysis, in which:

> links are formed with numbers of other mental sciences, the investigation of which promises results of the greatest value: links

with mythology and philology, with folklore, with social psychology and the theory of religion. (Freud, 1916–1917, p. 167)

He then explained that:

> [in] all these links, the share of psycho-analysis is in the first instance that of giver and only to a less extent that of receiver. It is true that this brings it *an advantage in the fact that its strange findings become more familiar when they are met with again in other fields*; but on the whole, it is psycho-analysis which provides the technical methods and the points of view whose application in these other fields should prove fruitful. (Freud, 1916–1917, p. 168, *my emphasis*)

In contrast to Jung, he could not, therefore, envision mutual input, on either the epistemological, methodological, or conceptual plane, something which must raise questions for us regarding his genuine interest for society and culture. And yet he devoted numerous works to it. This is to say that he had, all the same, rather many other reasons for being interested, in particular, that concerning the major role played by society and culture, or formulated otherwise in his metapsychology, by "reality" and the "external world", in the construction of every person's differentiated psychic apparatus, determining his or her humanisation and conditioning his or her socialisation, something partially accounted for, according to my personal research, by the notion of *Kulturarbeit* that he introduced beginning with *The Interpretation of Dreams*. In fact, I think that very early on he perceived and understood the relations of interdependence and interpenetration between the two domains—individual and collective, psychic and sociocultural—without being able *either to formulate them or to conceptualise them in that way*, because he was inspired by the individual/society antagonism, prevailing in the social and intellectual ideology of his time, something that can also help us understand his *transition and his rough transfer of concepts of individual psychology to mass psychology*.

What society and of what culture are we talking about?

Was it, in fact, *his* society, the Viennese society in which he grew up, lived, and created psychoanalysis? As for *his* culture, we could distinguish between the one he belonged to and the one that served as a reference. Thus, according to Anzieu (1987), he belonged to Jewish culture, that of the liberal Viennese bourgeoisie, more specifically that of the scientific and medical milieu, and to the Germanic culture, while he readily made reference to Greco-Roman culture.

However, like every thinker of his time, he asked himself about Western society and civilisation, experiencing critical periods generating "discontent" and change. Just as he was interested in historical and "primitive" societies from the evolutionist perspective of the British anthropologists of his time, which enabled him to fabricate a myth telling of the conditions of the creation of human culture, *culture in itself*, with its primordial institutions and social organisation, by establishing the Oedipus complex in its foundations.

So, when Freud dealt with society, culture, civilisation, the masses, or the community, I consider it necessary to take into consideration an interrelationship between these different levels: contemporary Viennese and Western, historical and primitive, finally the general categories of society, culture, and civilisation.

Freudian society and culture

In the first place, society and culture prove to be omnipresent and omnipotent for us, both in psychoanalysis and in Freud's life's work, in particular, through "reality" and the "external world", terms belonging to metapsychological language, on the basis of which the ego is differentiated from the id of every individual and, correlatively, the substitution of the reality principle for the pleasure principle effected what Freud considered to be a "psychic revolution", leading to the transformation of the pleasure-ego into a reality-ego. These expressions principally designate sociocultural reality and less frequently nature or material reality. Society and culture are the sources and places of "external real necessity", of the "power of the present", of constraints, demands, and "failure to provide satisfaction", but also of drive satisfaction and of actions, particularly aiming at adaptations, modifications, even mastery and sought-after satisfaction. From that point on, they will compel each person to engage in ongoing psychic work, throughout his or her entire life.

Furthermore, as his writings progress, Freud presents *evolving personal conceptions*, independent of the theorising of the sociologists and anthropologists who were his contemporaries, among whom may be cited: Durkheim and Mauss, leaders of the French school of sociology, who revolutionised sociology; and, in Germany, Weber, Tonnïes, Simmel, in particular; while among the anthropologists, the English school, with Tylor, Frazer, then with Rivers and Seligmann, was dominant.

It is a matter of socio-anthropology that is *psychoanalytic in essence*, both through its epistemological foundations, its method, and through its conceptual language, which fails to take into account the distinctiveness of the functioning and the singular products of this *other reality*, which is just as complex as psychic reality, *systemic* and *symbolic* in nature, and shot through with multiple antagonisms, as Durkheim and Mauss discovered and maintained in exemplary fashion. Indeed, Durkheim found that generally, and up until that time, sociologists, but also the English school of anthropology, as well as Wundt's *Elemente Völkerpsychologie*, had only viewed social phenomena as derived—that is to say, extended and generalised—mental facts. However, he established the existence of a line of demarcation between the former and the latter analogous to that separating the biological realm from the mineral realm, and he laid down the rule that a social phenomenon can only be produced by another social phenomenon, as well as establishing the principle of the interdependence of these phenomena then forming a *system*.

Considering then that English anthropology was not a social science, he envisaged introducing the sociological method into it—an idea adopted and applied by Malinowski and Radcliffe-Brown—and by imposing this, he thus hastened anthropology's transition to another phase of its history, in particular to functionalism, precisely that developed by Radcliffe-Brown and Malinowski, which was later adopted by British social anthropology.

From this perspective, the spirit of Freudian socio-anthropology was in line with that of English anthropology which, by the way, greatly inspired *Totem and Taboo*. Freud in fact borrowed from it, principally: its system of construction of insufficiently scrutinised, imprecise sociocultural facts taken out of their social context; the explanation– interpretation consisting of always finding the individual mental processes one believes to be the basis of social facts, something which converged with the hypotheses he wished to validate; their mode of reconstructing the past, a history not attested to by any document, in short, the writing of historical novels.

However, in other respects, Freudian thought reveals itself to be a product of historically and socioculturally determined thought that shows evidence of certain social and ideological representations prevalent in his time, but also in Viennese society undergoing a serious crisis. Let me indicate, in particular, the radical antagonism between individual and society, as well as the evolutionist ideology, in its developmental version (the development of society is comparable to that of an individual) and progressive version (evolution is animated by the progress sustained by the triumph of raison, dogma prevailing during the nineteenth century and appropriated by the liberal bourgeois members of *his* society).

So it is that I have detected an evolving progression of his discourse inherent to the very evolution of psychoanalytic doctrine, be it the theory of drives or of the psychic apparatus, for example.

This is why, I shall distinguish between two periods:

- That of the first topic, with some major texts, including *Three Essays on the Theory of Sexuality* (1905d); "'Civilized' sexual morality and modern nervous illness" (1908d), and *Totem and Taboo* (1912–1913).
- That of the second topic, dominated by three texts, but to which I shall add a fourth: "A short account of psycho-analysis" (1924f); *The Future of an Illusion* (1927c), *Civilization and its Discontents* (1930a) and *Moses and Monotheism: Three Essays* (1939a).

First period

Very early on, Freud defended the thesis of the *libidinal drive foundations* of culture that he would later define as his "psychic capital", which is not very surprising for a psychoanalyst unaware of socioanthropological theorisations! Indeed, as early as the *Three Essays on the Theory of Sexuality* (1905d), cultural productions are a matter of acquired sexual components, forces of sexual drives diverted from their sexual aim and directed towards new, non-sexual aims, through the process of sublimation, individual as well as collective.

In so doing, he affirmed, on the one hand, that this process partici-
pates in the constitution of culture and, on the other hand, that it is
a matter of production that is collective through the participation of
each of its members. Consequently, these drive components, sublimated or inhibited, even repressed, with respect to their aim, objects
of forms of renunciation and refashioning, represent the "culture's
psychic capital", which must necessarily take a great quantity of psychic energy away from the sexuality of its participants for its own
needs of consumption. This economic, drive approach of culture is
also particularly manifest in his "sexual morality" of 1908. While a
culture is generally built upon the repression of drives, it is also a
question of each person's personal gift of a part of his or her drive
capital, libidinal, and hostile motions, which will therefore represent
every individual's contribution to the constitution of this "common
cultural property in material and ideal goods", as a genuine partici-
pant in the constitution of the culture in question, which is a *collective
enterprise and common property*. This very notion of "common cultural property" would be neglected during the second period. In addition, he emphasised that *through the repression and displacement of
drives, normal sexuality would bring the culture to advance*, in contrast
to the perverse deviations in conflict with it through their incapacity
to mobilise these sexual components. Moreover, Freud plainly states
that a drive's "cultural value" lies in its capacity for displacement of the
object and aim.

In *Totem and Taboo*, through analogy with the neurotic symptom-
atic formations, the primordial institutions have an "animal" origin in
drives. They appertain to drive conflicts in the species that are oedipal
in nature, and constitute compromise social solutions to the problem
of wish compensation. Realised collectively, they represent "goods of
humanity".

But above all, his method led him to set up the ambivalent paternal side of the Oedipus complex at the foundation of culture, then as
an agent of liaison between the two fields—intrapsychic–individual and
collective, sociocultural—from a certain number of needs, capacities,
and processes of human mental activity, but also taking into consideration an essential analogy between the individual and society, that of

a psyche—individual, in the former case, and mass in the latter—within which we inevitably find similar processes. Individual psyche and culture are correlative, therefore interdependent.

Finally, the introduction of the notion of a "mass psyche" ensuring the continuity of psychic life between the generations is an extension of Wundt's notion of collective psyche as an extension of the individual psyche. It displays similarities with that of "collective consciousness" introduced by Durkheim (1893). As I have already formulated it, this pertains to the culture and represents an instance of it by referring to "human mental activity". It does not stand in a relationship of identity with the individual psyche, as group psychoanalysts have shown well, contrary to what Freud had imagined. In fact, its processes and its formations are distinctive of it, even though some analogies exist between these two psychic realities: individual and collective.

Second period

Freud's "A short account of psycho-analysis" (1924f) presents culture as the domain of expression of "human mental activity", presupposing a projective activity of external "shaping" of an internal world involving three portions corresponding to three areas of its representation of culture:

- combat with reality, nature, determining a community of work and interests of libidinously linked human beings, and a correlative social life
- the substitutive satisfactions of repressed wishes, figuring among them myths, literary and artistic creations
- the major institutions that enable mastery of the Oedipus complex and the individual libido's transition from its infantile liaisons to wished for social liaisons.

Then, with *The Future of an Illusion* (1927c) and *Civilization and its Discontents* (1930a), Freud plunges us into an elaborate description and exposes us to some structural antagonisms between culture or society and its members, as well as to paradoxes intrinsic to the culture or society itself.

First of all, he paints a picture for us of the overall culture involving, once again, three areas:

- The *material aspects* proceeding from two types of activities, those that are useful, vital in nature, enabling the acquisition and fabrication of goods and referring to the "material culture" and those that are useless, but nevertheless necessary to human beings, among them beauty, order, and cleanliness.
- The *"intellectual" aspects or "psychic goods"* integrating religious systems, philosophical speculation, artistic creations, as well as the formations of ideal or store of mankind's cultural ideals, and the human superego as "psychological cultural capital".
- Finally, what pertains to *modes of regulating social relations* ensured by ethics or morality, one of the expressions of the culture's superego, Freud would point out to us in *Civilization and its Discontents*, which produces its ideals and raises its demands.

What are its principal antagonisms and paradoxes? Paradoxes which are the source of conflicts and of ambivalence with regard to it?

Nature/culture antagonism

If the true foundation of the existence of the culture, which blends in with its principal task, consists of a community of work and human interests, associated together by identifications, aim-inhibited relations, and sublimated homosexual bonds, *essentially aiming at protecting them from the dangers of nature* and at dominating it in order to obtain vital goods, then it is also a *source of multiple forms of suffering* by the determining of a twofold coercion to work, both psychic (for example, sublimational) and social, individual, and collective, and by the instinctual renunciation required therefore engendering sacrifices.

The individual/society–culture antagonism

However, it is also threatened within by another source of danger: it must protect itself from its participants, human individuals endowed with "drives of animal origin", therefore, with what are called anti-social drives, sexual as well as destructive, that make virtual enemies of them, not to mention their narcissism, which must be held in check and changed into love of object, whence love as a factor of culture.

Freud ultimately identified two sources of hostility of individuals from which culture must protect itself:

- That inherent to the *animal nature* of human beings, constituted of "selfish", sexual and destructive, anti-social and anti-cultural drives, in search of satisfaction, and confronted with privations established by the basic prohibitions.
- That determined by the constraint to individual and collective work and the requisite drive renunciation, which engenders psychic sacrifices in its participants, determining a position virtually hostile to culture and its demands.

Its modalities of protection are also multiple: it must compensate those participating in it for the sacrifices of drive it imposes on them, by offering them "psychic goods", in fact, having this purpose, according to Freud, just like the institutions, devices, and commandments.

Nevertheless, culture's most determinant and meaningful method of protection against its participants' destruction drive—the most dangerous one—would be considered the establishment of the superego or conscience in each individual, thus becoming a "vehicle of the culture" and of the correlative advent of a sense of guilt. Culture, work of Eros, and serving it, goes hand in hand with this feeling of guilt, which inevitably induces a loss of happiness. This is the very purpose of *Kulturarbeit*, in both its individual and collective field.

For each society, it will therefore be a matter of finding modes of balancing these two sorts of demands: individual and collective.

Among the other "sociocultural" antagonisms that I have detected, I would like to indicate:

- that between women, as representing the interests of the family and of sexual life, and the culture;
- that between the family, from which young people must break away, helped in this task by the rites of puberty instituted by the society, and the culture;

- that between men and women in their relationship to the culture and to *Kulturarbeit*;
- that between *Kulturarbeit* and sexuality, through the necessary work of drive sublimation, which impoverishes the erotic drive capital, and its dangers of drive defusion;
- that between homosexual ties that are sublimated and inhibited with respect to the goal prevailing within the community of work and human interests, and the heterosexuality of conjugal bonds;
- that between sexuality as an autonomous source of pleasure and marriage:

> Society would impose upon all its members the same kind of genital sexual life based on a choice of one heterosexual object— therefore ruling out multiplicity of choice, the homosexual object and perversions—and a relationship between one man and one woman, principally procreative and indissoluble, within the framework of the institution of marriage.

But Freud also proposed a dynamic vision of culture as "process", work of Eros that *urges* human beings *to bond libidinally* amongst themselves in order to form great social units, all the while being subject to Ananke, real necessity, therefore, external reality. Consequently, Eros and Ananke are the parents of human culture. This process develops on the scale of humanity and seems analogous to individual development and to organic processes. Indeed, having to confront a major obstacle—the destructive instinct—it will therefore be a matter of a combat animated by necessary movements of fusion–defusion–refusion between Eros and this destructive instinct, corresponding thus to the essential content of life.

In *Moses and Monotheism*, Freud reminds us that at work in the psychic life of the individual are not only *contents experienced by himself or herself*, but also *innate contents*, "memory traces bound to an experience lived by earlier generations" continuing to persist as elements of phylogenetic origin and constituting an *archaic heritage*. For Freud, this notion of archaic heritage seems to represent *an agent of liaison between phylogenesis and ontogenesis* as well as individual and collective psychologies.

Moreover, if the foundations of the culture condition and favour— through the constraint of drive restrictions in particular—the outbreak of neurosis in its participants, and if the analogy between cultural development and that of the individual particularly based on certain similar processes presents a value, Freud allows himself to infer the possible existence of *neurotic* cultures and cultural eras under the influence "of tendencies of culture". Thus, culture produces individual neurosis, but also collective neurosis.

The Freudian notion of *Kulturarbeit*

It runs through all of Freud's work, from *The Interpretation of Dreams* onwards, even if it is not often designated as such. As I have identified it, this notion expresses the existence of relationships of interdependency and interpenetration between sociocultural and psychic and bodily individual realities. And the originality of Freudian thought is to have indicated to us the diverse modes of leaving its imprint and of individual transmission, bodily as well as intrapsychic, of what is cultural and social, as well as signifying to us that this *introjection of social aspects and of culture* conditions the constitution of a differentiated psychic apparatus, therefore the psychic hominisation of every individual that would permit his or her socialisation, therefore his or her incorporation into society, conferring upon him or her the status of "person" or of "subject". Thus, these subjects would participate in the collective work of a social nature, which is productive, preserving, and reproductive for their society and culture, their "common property".

By way of conclusion

With *methodological impertinence* which is historically determined, Freud would have established some foundations of a necessary psychoanalytic approach to *society* and *culture*, that would be taken up again and developed by other authors from varied perspectives. We may cite, in particular, Géza Róheim, Abram Kardiner, and Georges Devereux. I plan to pursue this exploration in the work of these authors as well as in that of contemporary authors. Nevertheless, it seems to me urgent, on the one hand, to elaborate a heuristic psychoanalytic methodology, which group psychoanalysts have initiated; on the other hand, to combine, within the framework of pluri- and interdisciplinary collaboration, the (individual and group) psychoanalytic approach to historical as well as to sociological, anthropological, and linguistic approaches within *the perspective of a genuinely pertinent and fruitful investigation of the complexity of this human reality.*

References

Anzieu, D. (1987). Influence comparée de la langue et de la culture françaises et germaniques sur l'auto-analyse de Freud [Comparative influence of French and Germanic language and culture on Freud's self-analysis]. *Psychanalyse à l'Université*, *12*(48): 525–540.

Assoun, P.-L. (1993). *Freud et les sciences sociales: psychanalyse et théorie de la culture* [*Freud and the Social Sciences: Psychoanalysis and Theory of Culture*]. Paris: Armand Colin.

Durkheim, E. (1893). *The Division of Labor in Society*. New York: Free Press, 1997.

Freud, S. (1900a). *The Interpretation of Dreams*. S. E., *4*: ix–627. London: Hogarth.

Freud, S. (1905d). *Three Essays on the Theory of Sexuality*. S. E., *7*: 123–246. London: Hogarth.

Freud, S. (1908d). "Civilized" sexual morality and modern nervous illness. *S. E.*, *9*: 177–204. London: Hogarth.

Freud, S. (1912–1913). *Totem and Taboo*. S. E., *13*: vii–162. London: Hogarth.

Freud, S. (1916–1917). *Introductory Lectures on Psycho-Analysis*. S. E., *15–16*. London: Hogarth.

Freud, S. (1924f). A short account of psycho-analysis. S. E., *19*: 189–210. London: Hogarth.

Freud, S. (1927c). *The Future of an Illusion*. S. E., *21*: 1–56. London: Hogarth.

Freud, S. (1930a). *Civilization and its Discontents*. S. E., *21*: 57–146. London: Hogarth.

Freud, S. (1939a). *Moses and Monotheism: Three Essays*. S. E., *23*: 1–138. London: Hogarth.

Wundt, W. (1912). *Elemente der Völkerpsychologie* [*Elements of Cultural Psychology*]. Leipzig: Alfred Kröner.

CHAPTER 3

The disappeared: a sorrow without dreams

Leopold Nosek

Introduction by João Seabra Diniz

At a time when we are frequently confronted with profound changes in the cultural environment, Leopold Nosek has very eloquently documented the importance of the culture that preceded us. The innovations of the present do not cancel out the experiences of the past. His lecture in 2016 at a national colloquium on freedom and fear had a great impact on the Portuguese community of psychoanalysts.

Progress in neurological knowledge is often seen as rendering previous conceptions obsolete. The author, speaking of ancient poets, underlines the importance of their role, "preserving the treasure of narratives that have made us who we are".

Regarding this tension between past and present in the field of science and culture in general, I think it is interesting to recall that Freud, still in the last years of the nineteenth century, wrote a text entitled "Entwurf einer psychologie", later translated into English as "Project for a scientific psychology" and only published after his death in 1950.

The historical summary of *The Standard Edition* (1950a [1887–1902]) quotes several letters to Fliess which show the deep concern attached to his goal of formulating a "psychology for neu-rologists". I quote one passage, among many significant ones:

> now that I have met with the neuroses ... I am vexed with
> two intentions: to discover what form the theory of psychi-
> cal functioning will take if a quantitative line of approach, a
> kind of economics of nervous force, is introduced into it, and,
> secondly, to extract from psychopathology a yield for nor-
> mal psychology. It is in fact impossible to form a satisfactory
> general view of neuro-psychotic disorders unless they can be
> linked to clear hypotheses upon normal psychical processes.
> (pp. 283–284)

It is a very expressive example of the concern of linking contemporary progress with the pathways of the past. As the author says near the end of his text, "we have all the ages of our personal development, with precocious phases continuing as our foundations and ever in a dual movement of altering and being altered by all that follows."

* * *

I

We learn from astrophysics that we see bodies in the universe that have already died, stars that have already disappeared. Although nonexis-tent, their light still reaches us crossing tremendous distances. We walk illuminated by the dead. They are stars that guide us as in other times they guided Melchior, Gaspar, and Balthazar. So to us is the figure of Homer—he speaks to us from an epoch in which Mnémosyne, goddess of memory and mother of the muses, still held her place in the Pantheon. The words of Homer preciously held in the memory and orally transmit-ted by those outliving him, ensure that the epic of human emancipation reaches us. Trained in the arts of the meter and the musical sonority of words, those early poets were thus preserving the treasure of narratives that have made us who we are.

The capacity to remember begins losing importance as the possibility of registering our memory through writing is consolidated. Mnémosyne becomes an anachronic goddess, and disappears from the Pantheon. *The Iliad* is then preserved as a written memory. How fairs it today, when we can carry an entire library on our mobile phones, research whatever and get instantaneous answers, or share on the social media sites the delectables we are devouring in our dining room? Can the focus of our memory be the pocket in which lies our electronic gadget? Will the instant become obsolete?

The classics are not to be kept in archives and libraries: they need to be seen anew at all moments. It is necessary that our memories be able to come to life again and take on the colour of who recovers them. This allows not only for their living but an individuality which reflects at once the times in which they are reborn and the subjectivity of the one taking on the classics. Whether or not we are aware of it, our tradition lingers in us in an incarnate form and is an essential part of what we believe we are.

I'm a nostalgic and insist on an unforgivable sin of our times: I suffer from depressive traits. I thus persist in recalling Homer and taking from *The Iliad* a passage that was once more known and revered. I continue believing in the importance of festivities, commemorations, and the ceremonials of mourning. We live in a civilisation that originates from two branches: Graeco-Roman and Judeo-Christian; that is, these cultures offer us narratives with which we delineate the trajectories of our lives. The stories of *The Iliad*, kept alive in the memory, afford the primordial Greek cities the substratum that makes way at their apogee for the development of poetry, theatre, philosophy, ethics; in sum, the values and practices which in the fourth century BC would culminate in the classic culture which still today underlies the narratives that guide us.

Marx saw the civilisations of the past as the childhood of humanity and as such, much like children, they could be unruly, impertinent, aggressive, shy, among many other characteristics. Within this spectrum, he said, the Greeks were healthy children and represented a precocious moment in the development of humanity. In Greek customs we find the infancy of what perhaps exists of the best in Western culture, what we could call with some degree of haughtiness a mature stage of social development.

Homer, in *The Iliad*, relates the lives of personages who yearned for a heroic death that would have them live on *in the mouths of men*. From this narrative I will take the death of Patroclus by Hector's sword, and the latter's own death vengefully perpetrated by Achilles. Let us recall that Homer's epic poem situates us in the passing from the archaic to the classical civilisation of the Greek polis; from this collection will arise in the agora the values of citizenship, honour, ethics, politics—that is, all the Greek manner of living. This narrative will structure the ways that are to enlighten us as a tradition. During Freud's time, classic literature was considered a key tool for any thinking worthy of consideration, and not so long ago Greek and Latin were mandatory in school curricula.

The narratives we possess shape us; further, they build humankind. Memory structured as poetry reveals the past and as such unveils the roots of the present, helping us in our attempt to understand our being or becoming within the whole. Recollection allows rediscovering these existences which preceded us and moulded us. It is not quite a matter of recovering the past but rather of recreating it. In this process we experience the passage of time and form an intuition of temporality.

In the first empirical science—for the Greeks, medicine—anamnesis, that is, recollection, is the initial act of medical intervention and the first act towards any possibility of healing. So it is now. On the other side, amongst the Greeks, the idea of death was associated with the passage of souls through the Lethe River, the river of forgetfulness or oblivion (the meaning of the word *lethe*). Psychoanalysis also has, in its origin, the practice of recollection and at its beginnings took on the idea of illness as a submission to rejected memories which, in the impossibility of being invoked, would trigger the appearance of monsters.

My proposal is that we begin looking at our disappeared in the light of other "dead stars". We need to search for answers even if they are insufficient and provisional as after all we are made of the very same human stuff as our remote ancestors. My one hope is to collaborate so that they do not get lost in the misdirections of our memory.

II

In a battle, Hector, prince of Troy, kills Patroclus, the friend of the Greek hero Achilles. Throughout the story the laments of the Greeks and of Achilles are heard, and throughout Book XXIII ("Prizes in honor of Patroclus") the mourning rites and homages to the dead are related.

They are accounts—the first known to us—of games and sports competitions held important in the Greek culture. Making up the homages are the car race, boxing match, wrestling, armed fight, shot puts, bow shooting, dart throwing, and the foot race, this last, by the way, won by Ulysses, who beats "swift-footed" Achilles.

We see well here not only the valuing of the nascent sports games but also the essential role allotted to funeral ceremonies. There had already been a banquet in honour of the dead. A grand pyre had been prepared and in the fire were burned the sacrificial animals. The fire burned all night with the help of the winds. The ashes were put in a golden urn and a burial mound was built for Patroclus. Only then did the games begin with grand prizes offered by Achilles. All of Book XXIII echoes with the pain of death, of friendship, and of reverence for the dead.

In the preceding Book, Homer had told of the battle waged between the Greeks and Trojans over the possession of Patroclus' corpse. A great dishonour it would be to abandon him to the wrath of the enemies; never would they allow that he serve as food to "the dogs and vultures of Troy". The Greek warriors launch with fury into the long battle told in Book XVII ("The heroic feats of Menelaus"), on seeing that:

> Hector had stripped Patroclus of his armour, and was dragging him away to cut off his head and take the body to fling before the dogs of Troy. (Book XVII, pp. 125–127)

The battle is fierce and continues throughout Book XVII:

> Thus did they fight as it were a flaming fire; it seemed as though it had gone hard even with the sun and moon, for they were hidden over all that part where the bravest heroes were fighting about the dead son of Menoetius ... (Book XVII, pp. 366–369)

The list of the dead is long, be it among the Greeks or the warriors of Troy. Something deems it imperative to fight with all their might for the body and the rites of mourning. The many dead on both sides are worth the exchange for the mortal remains of Patroclus. Great is the space that the story of Achilles, Patroclus, and Hector occupies in this founding epic poem, covering a sequence of nine books, from XVI to XXIV, the last in *The Iliad*: Book XVI: "Patroclus' feats"; Book XVII: "The heroic feats of Menelaus"; Book XVIII: "The making of arms"; Book XIX: "Fury takes over"; Book XX: "The battle of the gods"; Book XXI: "The battle along the river"; Book XXII: "The retreat of Hector"; Book XXIII: "Prizes in honor of Patroclus"; Book XXIV: "The rescue of Hector". What makes the death of so many heroes in exchange for a dead body worth it?

Upon Patroclus' death, Achilles, filled with rage, kills Hector. Blinded by pain over the loss of his friend, Achilles takes Hector's corpse to the Greek camp and for nine days, always in the mornings, puts himself to the task of humiliating the mortal remains: he drags the body three times each day around Patroclus' grave. The gods observe all and show they are displeased over the disrespect for the dead. It is thanks to their intervention that the body dragged across the camp, while violently insulted, remains unharmed. Apollo summons the gods and these abandon the idea of sending Hermes to rescue the corpse. Apollo intervenes highly upset by Achilles:

> Even so has Achilles flung aside all pity, and all that conscience which at once so greatly banes yet greatly boons him that will heed it. (Book XXIV, pp. 44–45)

Hermes goes then to Priam, the mourning father of Hector, and orients and guides him to make the impracticable crossing over the Greek front to speak with Achilles.

We are to reach here one of the most beautiful passages of *The Iliad*, worthy ever of being revisited. Continuing thus with this impossible summary, we now find Priam before Achilles, who is stunned by this sudden appearance. We are at verse 476 of Book XXIV and I specify this to encourage the reader to go through these passages on their own, free from the violence done to the text for the purposes of my argumentation, and open to the infinite aesthetic pleasure that the reading of the original affords. Be it as it may:

> King Priam entered without their seeing him, and going right up to Achilles he clasped his knees and *kissed the dread murderous*

hands that had slain so many of his sons. (Book XXIV, pp. 476–478,
my emphasis)

Homer, magnificent, relates to us Priam's plea which bestirs in Achilles
thoughts of his own father's worrying and yearning for him in his
absence due to war. Both weep bitterly for their losses and Achilles is
greatly impressed with the old man's daring. In fact, both feel in their
encounter the quasi divine power of their figures and respect each
other … Achilles acquiesces to giving back Hector's body, ceding to the
gods' will that it be so. Priam, in a demonstration of respect, fills Achilles
with rich gifts.

Achilles then invites Priam to dine with him and has him spend the
night so that he may leave in peace the following day with his son's body.
He further offers him a twelve-day war truce for the proper grieving
and funeral rites of Hector to take place. Troy may thus mourn its son
and hero and pay him homage, a custom taken on since the primitive
Greeks and which becomes a sign of civilisation, no matter the degree of
violence practised in war:

> When they had heaped up the barrow they went back again
> into the city, and being well assembled they held high feast in
> the house of Priam their king. Thus, then, did they celebrate the
> funeral of Hector tamer of horses. (Book XXIV, pp. 800–803)

So ends *The Iliad*, not in the triumph of the renowned and nonexistent
horse of Troy (this passage does not appear in any Homeric narrative,
as was discovered belatedly), but in the triumph of the mourning ceremony being carried through properly. And here once again I cannot fail
to perceive that we are moving through fundamental roots of Western
civilisation. How could we forget?

III

Returning to the reference to Marx made at the start, I would like to
recall also the beautiful final passage of his Preface and Introduction to
A Contribution to the Critique of Political Economy, a text of 1857 that

is part of a rough draft that was never completed. Discovered in 1902 among Marx's manuscripts, it proposes themes which he intended to develop on later:

> A man cannot become a child again, or he becomes childish. But doesn't he enjoy the child's naiveté, and mustn't he strive to reproduce its truth on a higher level himself? Doesn't the special character of every epoch come alive in its true nature in the nature of its children? Why shouldn't the historical childhood of humanity, in which it attained its most beautiful development, exert an eternal charm as a stage that will never recur? There are unruly children and precocious children. Many of the ancient peoples belong to this category. The Greeks were healthy children. The charm of their art for us does not contradict the undeveloped stage of society on which it grew. Rather it is its result and is inseparably connected with the fact that the immature social conditions in which it arose and in which alone it could arise can never recur. (Marx, 1976, p. 32)

The question that precedes the above paragraph will never cease to be intriguing: why does this ancestral epic continue to provide aesthetic pleasure and ethical education? Why is what *The Iliad* presents us with so stunning a reality?

What is Achilles before the power which technology provides? What is Hermes before the gods of commerce of our times? To which entity or nation would Olympus correspond today? What speed would we attribute to Apollo? Hera's wisdom would belong to which university? Or yet: who is Zeus compared with Google? In the childhood of humanity was born the épopée, the epic of heroic grandeur. In the modern novel we find human frailty; the suffering in a world of forces the individual does not control and before whose mysteries he stoops. It is a subjective drama in which there is not the help of a mythology such as that which allowed the Greek hero to understand and accept his fate.

On the other hand, for us it no longer makes sense to think of time as linear and even less as running an ascending course—this is no more than an anthropomorphic time, wherein we have births, developments, declines, and death. We will be more attuned if we think of interpenetrating times, times in whose diversity there coexist different moments of maturation. It is more suitable to think of watches that move in distinct times and speeds, times harmonic and contradictory, synchronistic and diachronic, archaic and contemporary. It would be useful to think of these multiple hands moving in a type of emptiness, without our visualising the numbers which define the hours. Times moved also by desires and utopias and which, pointing towards a future dimension, can bring us, as in a glimpse, an apprehension of the present.

If I read *The Iliad* today it is evidently impossible that I see it as a Greek or Renaissance man would. When read, each historic moment imprints the signs of its existence. Further, within it will also be present my own personal times of development. There are authors who think of the Renaissance as the height of the Middle Ages. Then others see it as the rebirth of the classic apogee. Still others view it as a time of rupture, as the emergence of the modern man in his infancy. Perhaps all these times coexist simultaneously with times that escape our perception and, why not? The ages and cultures interpenetrate.

As such, for us psychoanalysts childhood does not belong to a past to be unveiled. We do not look on the memories of the past as parasites that try making themselves present obscuring our perception of the moment. We think, of infancy as the cornerstone upon which is built the edifice of our personal culture: this internal ecology is what our existence is based on. The Greeks, among other "healthy children", lay the groundwork for our mode of being. On this foundation new constructions may arise and be developed. I can think of my own self in this reflection as at a certain point of development—a point where my end is more visible to me—which in a way renews in me the wonder at times of the presence and the absence of the body, the constructs of poetry on love, abandonment, the joy of creation, and the infinite mystery of death, at the poetic construction of mourning.

I must say that today, bewildered by the issue of the disappeared, I discover a new *Iliad* which is of a peculiar beauty, in which the inevitable search of a body presents itself to me as an enigma. From this great star we inherited from Homer a light wakens now for my consideration: the respect for death and the need of the concrete presence of the body of the dead.

In view of the technical resources at our disposal today, the absence of the dead can be situated in the scenario of a vast process of defrauded mourning. We have been compelled to live with the absence of the millions of dead in an industrialised holocaust. The dead turned to smoke and dust wandering this earth. In Latin America today we go on living with this interrogation over the thousands of political "disappeared" the different dictatorships inflicted on us. Mothers, fathers, and relations dedicate their lives in search of the remains of a presence whose existence is denied at the very moment in which is denied their death. In this search they become witnesses not only to the verity of that individual presence, but also of a tragic moment in history.

Yet still, once again: what originates these wanderers who perambulate in search of signs which will add nothing to the knowledge already established about their deaths? What need is it that perpetuates this eternal search? Which marks of mourning are borne by those not given the benefit conceded to Achilles and Priam; that is, the possibility of grieving over the body of Patroclus and Hector? Why do the gods become indignant concerning the torture inflicted to Hector's body by Achilles gone mad with the desire for vengeance?

These are the very gods who arm the Greeks to defeat Troy, yet there is something which surpasses the law governing them: profanation and disrespect for the body, or—what an Ancient Greek would not even cogitate—the disappearance of the dead. For what reason do the best warriors and heroes launch into battle, willing to die for the rotten remains of an anatomy?

This need for mourning makes us who we are. Our alternative would be to become something else, perhaps the stuff of which the dead are made. There is a passage from body matter to matter of the memory, to the matter that constitutes our spirit, or, more broadly, the stuff of which our culture, our art, our knowing, and our ethics are made, the same which permeates all our personal and social makeup. Going back in time, I refer to the fifth century BC Greek lyric poet, Pindar, from whom I take direction:

> Creatures of a day! What is man?
> What is he not? A dream of a shadow
> Is our mortal being. But when there comes to men
> A gleam of splendour given of heaven,
> Then rests on them a light of glory
> And blessed are their days. (*Pythian 8*)

I skip forward almost two millennia and read in Shakespeare (2006) what Prosperous teaches us in *The Tempest*: "We are such stuff as dreams are made on". Having these ideas for roots, I see no alternative but to search in Freud; after all, what stuff are we made of? How is our spirit constructed? How are dreams built? Why do we care about dead stars, memories? Poetry and dreams, in their depths, have they not their equivalences?

Walter Benjamin takes on the reflections in *Beyond the Pleasure Principle* (Freud, 1920g) and cites from the Freudian essay: "Consciousness does not register any traces of memory", and "Consciousness arises in the place of the mnemic trace". Consciousness is thus:

> characterised by the peculiarity that the excitation process does not leave in it, as it does in all other psychic systems, a permanent alteration of its elements, but is as it were discharged in the phenomenon of becoming conscious and vanishes. (Freud, 1920g, p. 4)

Memory records are in their turn "strongest and most enduring when the process that imprints them never reached consciousness at all" (Benjamin, 1987, p. 204). Translating Freud into Proustian terms, Benjamin writes: "Only what has not happened to the subject as a living experience can become a component of involuntary memory" (Benjamin, 1987, p. 212).

Which means that no else turns into the patrimony of the unconscious, or unconscious knowledge, than what breaks through the protective barrier against the traumatic provided by consciousness—and in the painful process of the rupture of this membrane is left a mark of experience. Here a clear difference is established between experience and lived experience. Upon this experience the psyche will continue its process attempting to reach an inner equilibrium, a quiescence, a homeostatic repose. It will try to placate the pain creating pathways for this rupture, starting off the dream processes. There will now simultaneously be an access from this "erasure" to consciousness and thus the emergence of the possibility of control of the traumatic. In this process of oneiric creation both the territories of the unconscious and consciousness are built, for the dream has a face turned to each one of these regions of the spirit; the construction of these territories will be made by juxtaposition of the dream elements and their settlement, through figurations. The building and settling of the spirit will ensue inevitably from an excessive and painful experience which will be organised from the stuff of which dreams are made of, the stuff of our existence.

A vast territory of reflection opens before us on the importance and character of the aesthetic experience, of artistic creation in the building of learning and the elaboration of humanity in culture and daily living. I recall Raymond Williams' assertion that "culture is ordinary"—culture is the prosaic, the day-to-day, the shoes we wear, how we move in the world. Art is not delight: it is excess that calls us to surviving the aesthetic stimulus, to having art as experience.

I point out here the contrast between journalistic information which juxtaposes data not differentiated in emotional intensity, and the narrative, which imposes on us the effort of following on the experience it brings us. Information has a beginning and an end, it is complete, and unlike the narrative, does not have us seeking its continuity. The dream also does not enclose a meaning in itself, it does not disclose information within it—it is much more a provisional meaning heading in search of the next meaning. We are not upset when seeing news that is very grave juxtaposed with the scoring of a soccer goal. Such is, actually, the typical scheme in which being informed coincides with being alienated.

In another way is construed a narrative, a poetic or aesthetic structure. Let us recall that a fundamental source of our ethics lies in Sophocles, in his tragedy of the children of Oedipus. It is the dilemma of Antigone who meets death on not hesitating in burying her brother Polynices. Her dilemma is between loyalty to the law of the city and the law of her own conscience.

IV

The territory of this reflection is like no other, which I must say began in informal conversations with interviewers of the Comissão da Verdade (Truth Commission), responsible for investigating the happenings and experiences of the victims of the military dictatorship in Brazil. One of the questions that came up was: why is it that in this country there have been no productions (up to now, at least) of relevant literary or film works on this period? As we see it, most of the works that have come to the general public are either in the journalistic or cathartic vein. One of the hypotheses we brought up was the absence of a real rupture with the dictatorship; there would have been an accommodation ignoring the potentially traumatic elements of that transition.

I proceed with the argument turning now to Freud's essay "Mourning and melancholia" (1917e). The starting point is the idea that there is no representation of death in the unconscious, being that our fear of death dislocates to other territories. Let us think, for example, about the old custom of building family tombs in cemeteries in order to rest together as a family group. We want to stay near those we love—the fear of death expresses itself in the sphere of helplessness, loneliness, and abandonment. Think on the identity between the idea of the body being cremated and the claustrophobic phantasy, and so many other unconscious phantasies interwoven with this grand unknown which is death. Not to speak of the religious concepts of eternal life, reincarnation, and others, so varied as are cultures and religions. In the Greek world, the dead went to a specific region after crossing Lethe, the river of oblivion. How many ceremonies have we not invented precisely to avoid forgetting our dead?

Thus, if the concept of death is unbearable to us, what is mourning about? Freud related the mourning process to the phenomenon of melancholia. The latter is linked with the refusal to abandon the lost loved object. This object would maintain its presence by means of the melancholic remembering. Melancholy turns the object eternally present and would be a dysfunction in the process of mourning. Succinctly, in the mourning process the object lost in the external world becomes a presence in the internal world, in the spirit of the one who suffered the loss. We no longer have whom we love: now we are whom we love. The hatred set off by the loss accommodates itself. We develop an identification with what we lost. In this working-through, a paradox sets in: the spirit is enriched and achieves this via tragic routes. As always, in Freud, what begins as a psychopathologic analysis becomes a universal process of construing and settling of the spirit. The pathology migrates to a theory of the spirit, towards a psychology in itself.

I think we need the body to be able to bear this quasi impossible task of mourning. So that free from the shadow of the one departed, life may go on. During the funeral ceremony tragic moments intersperse with moments of calm. When the body is brought to the site there is a commotion; there follows a quietude, and then another grave moment when the coffin is closed. In the process, again, the calm gives way to displays of pain, of sorrow, when the body goes down into the earth. After this follow days of elaborate ceremonials in rites which vary from culture to culture. It is as though we need to give life to the body that is present to allow us to have, time and again, the renewed experience of loss.

When what we have is not the dead but rather the disappeared, not even melancholy can settle in. What will exist is a vacuum, a hollow, a hole in the spirit, a dead space that like a black hole will attract to it all that is alive. It works as a parasitic structure that corrodes, that blocks thinking, the affects, introducing deformations in the pathways of the soul, impeding life from going on.

At the cultural and historical levels there will occur the same deformations that befall the individual fates. Culture is kept from moving ahead with its trajectory, it is impoverished and can engender monstrosities. I like always recalling what Antonio Candido (1948), citing Otto Rank, said of literature: that it is humanity's dream. It has nothing at all to do with journalistic platitudes. Literature, like dreams, deals with the memory which rent consciousness and planted itself in us with a conscious face and an unconscious face, with infinite associative routes in its territory. The narrative also breaks through consciousness and will always be able to take in new glimmers of the "involuntary memory". What we have in the constructs of culture we also have in our individual trajectories. We have all the ages of our personal development, with precocious phases continuing as our foundations and at any time in a dual movement of altering and being altered by all that follows.

I tried showing how the archaic hero Achilles and his *entourage* have shaped us and shape the present, as they do our culture, our way of living, our relationships, and our yearnings. We can no longer seek the heroic death of epic heroes, we do not have their certainties. We seek much more keenly what would be our meaning. We search for a meaning which (supposedly) was lost.

* * *

Those that dictatorships represented denied the pain and the loss. They did not want the rupture and managed to brush it away from those who needed it. Those who were opposed did not have the power to make themselves heeded or preferred to accommodate, and our disappeared were kept from existing even as the disappeared. They became the exemplary symptom of a political accord that was made, impeding any mourning or even a possible melancholy from happening. Losses were not registered. History had to go on and keep quiet. The Comissão da Verdade saw itself limited in its work, duly touched up. How can we not think that these authoritarian, retrograde remains have not tainted the political agreements that followed and that they are not at the roots of deformities which today explode as dystopias in our society?

These holes in our thoughts, these veilings of the truth, these denials of the truth, affect all, the whole of society. In the break with democracy, in the years of obscurity, and of loss truly experienced, the arts survived. During the dictatorship when the truth could exist even clandestinely, dreams could be built. Without the absence of truth, dreams could exist. It may well be that this crisis moves toward other figures and social sectors. It may be other globalised protagonists will arise, waiting only for a breakdown or a crisis to come on the scene. We will have other historical movements, for sure, but our disappeared will continue to haunt us. Just as our slave past is a daily phantasm that devastates us in the privacy of our homes. To deny the narrative of the tragic in history is to inevitably feed the phantasms. Taking advantage of our obscurities, they will not miss out on the chance to reappear.

References

Benjamin, W. (1987). O narrador: considerações sobre a obra de Nikolai Leskov [The narrator: considerations on the work of Nikolai Leskov]. In: S. P. Rouanet (Trans.), *Walter Benjamin: Obras Escolhidas I. Magia e técnica, arte e política. Ensaios sobre literatura e história da cultura* [*Walter Benjamin: Selected Works I. Magic and Technique, Art and Politics. Essays on Literature and History of Culture*]. São Paulo: Brasiliense.

Candido, A. (1948). La figlia che piange [The crying daughter]. In: *O observador literário* [*The Literary Observer*]. São Paulo: Imprensa Oficial do Estado/ Conselho Estadual de Cultura, 1959.

Freud, S. (1917e). Mourning and melancholia. *S. E., 14*: 237–258. London: Hogarth.

Freud, S. (1920g). *Beyond The Pleasure Principle*. S. E., *18*: 1–64. London: Hogarth.

Freud, S. (1950a [1887–1902]). Project for a scientific psychology. S. E., *1*: 281–391. London: Hogarth.

Marx, K. (1976). *Preface and introduction to A Contribution to the Critique of Political Economy*. Peking: Foreign Languages Press [original in German, 1859].

Shakespeare, W. (2006). *A tempestade* [*The Tempest*], B. Heliodora (Trans.). Rio de Janeiro: Nova Aguilar.

Special sources used for English version of Nozek's work

Excerpts from Homer's *The Iliad*, translated by Samuel Butler (Encyclopedia Britannica, Inc).

Marx's *Introduction to A Contribution to the Critique of Political Economy*, text taken from Foreign Languages Press, prepared for the internet by David J. Romagnolo

Pindar's *Pythian 8*, translated by Richard Stoneman (London: Everyman Library).

CHAPTER 4

Virtual space, identity, and psychoanalysis: a new world or a dreadful voyage?*

Andrea Marzi

Introduction by Rui Aragão Oliveira

Andrea Marzi, a psychoanalyst from the Italian Psychoanalytical Society, came to Lisbon in 2017 to take part in a necessary debate which had been growing in intensity over the last decade: the vast adoption of highly sophisticated technological tools and the development of unconscious mental functioning.

An attentive researcher of the subject since the beginning of this century, participating and coordinating international reference editions, he frames the subject within the debate of psychoanalytical ethics, having also provided a unique contribution in Italy to the newly revised discussion on confidentiality in the analytical clinic in times of remote communicational uses.

This work is a meta-psychoanalytic reflection on the organisation of cyberspace and identity construction. It takes technological

---

*This article is a reviewed version of the text presented in the workshop with the same title held in Lisbon, at the Sociedade Portuguesa de Psicanálise, 11 February 2017.

omnipresence as its starting point and leads into a broad discussion that relates virtual space with the space of psychic reality.

In this text, Andrea Marzi invites us to explore the vicissitudes that the fluidity of modernity places before us, and which he studies in depth in his book *Psychoanalysis, Identity, and the Internet: Explorations into Cyberspace* (2016).

The notions of one's own space, corporeality, and identity, which are central to the history of psychoanalysis, have now become decisive fields of expansion.

Marzi then reveals how the study of cyberspace and human behaviour can be a valuable aid in deepening knowledge of mental functioning, and where the human sciences must assume an indispensable place in the debate to which he proposes to give impetus.

In the clinical exhibition he presents, Andrea Marzi also addresses technical implications associated with the role of the setting and the analytical field, which elegantly and carefully illustrates how the subject is already present in our consulting rooms, even if psychoanalysts have not always consciously been aware of this.

He deliberately tries not to position himself in the simple nosographic and normative position that differentiates between aspects of a more compulsive and disturbing nature (although it is understood that he necessarily takes them into account). Instead, he adopts a courageous position, which is evident in the clinical intervention that the text describes, where the analogy of the use of virtual space with that of Winnicottian potential space is clear, translating into a position that we consider pioneering in the exploration of aspects of the unconscious world.

This chapter by Andrea Marzi is an excellent initial contact to a problem that has become even more decisive in these dramatic times of a world pandemic.

* * *

On the internet every day we seek information, buy something, play video games, chat, work, and so on. What is the nature of the space we surf on and through? Is it virtual or real? What is the actual relation between virtual reality we inhabit more or less in a video game, or a film, or a common experience on the internet and the psychic reality that is one of the main foci of psychoanalysis? What about the corporeality, the time and space that we are accustomed to considering as the milestones of subjective experience? What happens to real relationships among people?

Actually, just as psychoanalysis reads the multifaceted nature of virtual reality, the reverse transpires, and cyberspace affects and influences seminal reflections about psychoanalysis itself and the virtual space of the mind.

It is, in fact, undeniable that the digital world, which produces interactions and disseminates information in a way that was unthinkable only a few decades ago, poses questions and problems for the scientific and humanistic disciplines, including ethics and psychoanalysis. It asks us to look into the issues of reality and truth, a theme that reverberates problematically for psychoanalysis and from which it can receive stimuli and, perhaps, clarification. It asks us to look into the bond that links materiality, immateriality, and virtuality, understood as space and/or potentiality. It poses questions imbued with emotion about the subject of permanence and transience, of memory, and its survival. It poses questions about the conservation and, conversely, the obliteration of testimony, catalogued and documented on the internet but at risk of disappearing, given its intrinsic fragility at times not governable by personal choices.

Undoubtedly, it is of seminal importance that the peculiar characteristics of the encounter with the particular state of mind of internet-addicted patients be explored, attempting to show in detail the path of the therapy, psychotherapeutic or analytic, and the relationship between the analyst and the net surfer, a castaway in virtual reality. But it is of even more relevance that we expand our reflections on a number of trends that seem absolutely unavoidable for psychoanalysis.

First of all, psychoanalysis needs to develop an enquiry into the nature of virtual reality, the world of informatics and the new media. In addition, a psychoanalytic enquiry which tackles the psychopathological levels of addiction, starting from the potential of risk inherent in immersion in cyberspace, is needed. Beyond this, we should develop a reflection, starting from cyberspace and using it as a perspective about psychoanalysis itself and the "virtual spaces" in the mind, their possible existence and meaning, their role within the setting, the consequences in the analytic field, and the distinctive characteristics of the analyst's meeting with an "internet-addicted" mind. Consequently, it would be of great importance to develop a comparison between virtual space, dream space, and some crucial concepts in psychoanalytical theorising (such as, for example, Bion's β-elements which can fill a space with a quality which can induce psychosis, or Winnicott's transitional space, and various autistic mechanisms). These are some of the most fruitful directions in which we can proceed if we want to increase the quality of our reflection on the complex world of digital technology.

Furthermore, this is why I tried to give a contribution on this subject, writing and editing a book (Marzi, 2013, 2016), as well as some national and international essays. Psychoanalysis cannot avoid such a crucial challenge.

Psychoanalysis and the digital world

It would be a mistake to think that the issues inherent in cyberspace and virtual reality have been neglected in the psychoanalytic field. In the span of the past twenty years, and at an increasing pace during the past decade, the psychoanalytic literature has been enriched with numerous contributions, from various viewpoints and under various forms, within the sphere of the International Psychoanalytical Association (IPA) and in other spheres relating to psychoanalysis. Among others, in witness to this is the monograph published by the *Psychoanalytic Review*, "Special issue on the Internet" (Eigen & Malater, 2007), and the Sixth British–Italian Dialogue (2011) with the title "Dream space and virtual space in the analytic process".

Growing attention, therefore, is being given to an argument that does not cease to arouse varied, sometimes extreme, feelings that range from enthusiastic approaches about cyberspace and virtual reality, to outright condemnation, demonisation, and anxiety-ridden scenarios. However, these points of view underwent a shift during the first decade of the twenty-first century.

In the IPA panel of 2001, "The impact of new technologies and new realities in psychoanalysis" edited by Suarez and Jasso (2002), there was a certain convergence of contrary and negative positions regarding the new media forms, and many authors insisted that there was a risky and negative relationship between the eruption of the digital era and the present-day world, a digital space where the power of individual and group narcissism is rampant, where people, and above all, children, are exposed to the transformation of human beings into consumers, consumed in their turn by increasingly intense sensory stimuli. In such a situation psychoanalysis would tend to lose its role, not being compatible with this pounding current of "liquidity". According to some authors, this would also result in dangerous implications for young minds in formation, which would be clouded by a passivity that does not help the capacity to think.

In 2010, at the time of the Chicago IPA Congress, the perspective changed, and authors placed greater attention on a variety of aspects existing within the "cyber" world, presenting more flexible viewpoints. Many of the authors showed that they were fully aware that the irruption of the digital world into the analytic process inevitably had repercussions in the aspects of privacy and intimacy inherent in analytic practice, raising questions for the ethical dimension as well as for the traditional authority of the analyst. In addition, it is also necessary to consider that technique frees us from certain limitations, but at the same time nails us to new forms of acquiescence.

Bonaminio and colleagues, for example (in the Chicago panel, 2010), suggested again the figure of an analyst who knows how to observe himself closely when faced with the impact that these new technologies have on the analyst and on psychoanalytic techniques. Bonaminio points out that such a technology, while generating the risk of greater fragmentation, can provide an opportunity, for the adolescent, to gain a greater sense of reality in the perception of himself as belonging to a group (in social networks, for example). It is therefore time to put behind us the phase of moralising oppositions, of apocalyptic disapproval on one hand, and a complete faith in the innovative potential of the new technologies on the other, and on the contrary to try to search for a more realistic position, using the internet as a helpful vantage point from which to revisit and compare psychoanalytic models and even to develop some new ones. We have the opportunity to investigate, among various subjects, whether the digital world, with its particular characteristics, may have an influence on our attitude toward symbolisation and on the theme of the construction of identity, and whether cyberspace interweaves with significant cross-references to the sense of analytic space, and to what extent it might do so.

Psychoanalysis and virtual reality

It is undoubtedly difficult to define the concept of "virtual". If we try to approach it from a psychoanalytic standpoint, virtuality might suggest something about the "mind" (as the object of our analytic work), in that both share the same character of place/non-place, having a base that is physical and material (the brain and the nervous system, or the structure of the hardware), and both are also dematerialised. Since it is not a truly existing space in a physically material sense, or one that is concretely visible and so perceptible to the human sensory faculties, virtual space seems to blatantly repropose the Kantian–Bionian concept of the impossibility of knowing the thing itself, that is, something that one can conceive of but not perceive. We grasp the manifestations derived from it, the symbolic images that are revealed, in this case, through the operations of the hardware and then the software up through the perception of our eyes and nervous system.

Indeed, it is possible to think that the mental space and the virtual space of cyberspace evoke each other (in a form of similarity or reciprocal allusion). The genetic referrability of the expression cyberspace (the computer place where virtual reality, the "virtual space", resides) to an invention of literary imagination[1] and, therefore, to a special aspect of human creativity further links these concepts with a Winnicottian perspective, the central concept of *potential space*. This is the subject's creative place that opens up a multifaceted dialogue with a virtual space of connections and divergences. This occupies a paradoxical third place (potential space) that overlaps with them, sharing their natures but also remaining distinct from them: we could think of it as the middle kingdom. This way of seeing brings into play diverse psychoanalytic models, which, nevertheless, can be found to be in agreement with respect to certain aspects, if thought of in this dimension.

As many authors in the analytic sphere point out, there is absolutely no doubt that the new technologies have an impact on the subject. The aspects

---

[1] The term cyberspace appears for the first time in the mid-1980s as a merger of the terms cybernetics and space. It was coined by William Gibson, the most representative author of the "Cyberpunk", to indicate an imaginary reality that is generated and lives in computer networks.

of the self, both intrapsychic and interpsychic (therefore, intersubjective) relations, are influenced and subjected to possible changes. This pertains to adults, but even more to children and adolescents because it is becoming increasingly clear that the digital world has an impact, in different ways and in different degrees, on the capacity not only to form mental representations, but also on the aptitude for symbolisation. As outlined above, we might go on to ask ourselves what the internet has produced and will be able to produce within psychoanalysis and, at the same time, what psychoanalysis will be able to do with the internet.

We can underline again that virtual reality (VR) and cyberspace do not correspond with one another, but they share a common space: we might say that VR is the language spoken in cyberspace. What is cyberspace made of? Of VR, we might say, and it certainly is, even if it is not only that: we might imagine this relationship with cyberspace as a container in which the content, according to what has been said so far, is represented by virtual objects, by VR precisely.

Moreover, it is possible to think that the mental space and the virtual space of cyberspace evoke each other (in a form of similarity or reciprocal allusion), since both are imagined as being endowed with a volume suited to welcoming specific contents of every nature: aspects, states of mind, fantasies, or numberless dematerialised objects.

Patients' communications about their experiences in cyberspace, implicating the diverse senses and sensoriality in all its forms—perception of colours, sounds, images, words—enable working-through within the analytic experience, thanks to the closeness of the dimensionality experienced and lived in these two spaces. In the analytic session, this material creates a *pabulum* from which unknown emotions—that can be given or re-given meaning—can spring, bound to a new construction of meaning.

In such a setting, we might postulate that the virtual condition brings an important contribution to the thinking process in analysis on acknowledging that full, satisfying, and genuine immersion can be realised only when the relational quality develops three-dimensionally, allowing contact to be achieved in each of the two worlds, virtual space and mental space, while maintaining that "correct distance" acceptable to the sense of one's own boundaries.

So, virtual space succeeds in being mental space (and *vice versa*, we might conjecture), when it is correlated with shared experiential zones (of exchange, of superimposition) if the subject succeeds in living this space as a place where "drafts of analytic thought" (Hautmann, 1999, p. 76) are possible, using cyberspace ("dreaming it") as a constant and flourishing source of thoughts.

Three-dimensionality, understood in the sense now suggested, makes it possible to effect analytic operations, with regard to space and to the (virtual) objects that exist in it. In these cases, the subject can connect up dispersed or, in any case, unorganised elements, *proto informatic elements*, I propose to call them, giving to them a form of life, experiences, original elaborations (even artistic ones), and adventures of the mind that are not imbued with omnipotence or destructive narcissism. These elements connect, instead of breaking up into fragments. They are emotional–affective products that are, in this way, endowed with meaning, with elaborative progress, reciprocal exchange, and a sense of limits.

The person who exchanges emotional–affective communications with the cyber world can draw on the symbolisation and constant production of what we might also call a "film of thought" (Hautmann, 1999), a forerunner of further developments. Here, what the subject detects in the digital world (which can be thought of as an accumulation of pre-symbolic or symbolic elements) can really trigger a "relational flow", the fruit of projective and introjective exchanges, aimed at the construction of new elements of thought, endowed with meaning.

Gianni is back

We are perfectly aware that the creative "virtuality" of the potential space not infrequently does not succeed in becoming dynamic, instead imploding into the concrete or even into something very close, for example, to the annihilating infinity of Bion's hallucinosis. Therefore, it can also be a space in which aspects of the subject's internal world can be experienced as concretely manipulable, resulting in considerable confusion between the internal and external worlds.

This immense and indefinite virtual space can be imagined, or used, for the acting out by subjects who, unable to use their own inner mental space, try their hand at exporting it to the outside, into virtual reality or cyberspace in short, using it as an extroversion of their self and from within oneself, and also as an attempt at trying to see their own psychic space in this way, to touch it with their hands.

Authors who have investigated the "new psychopathologies" have pointed out how, and how much, the various subjects can themselves broaden the virtual space of cyberspace with an essentially one-way projective flow. In particular, all the clinical cases described more or less bear witness to this trend, and offer a fascinating panorama that is profoundly stimulating for analytic thought.

Clinical reflection on a patient whom I will call Gianni, with whom I had an important analytic experience, allows me to propose and also highlight the opposite possibility, one that is decidedly unusual: the return from cyberspace of what can be thought of as a world of objects that had been evacuated there.

Gianni, a thirty-year-old chemist, suffered from an episode of marked depression during the period of his final high-school exams. This occurred again some years later, at the time he was getting his degree. His family includes a brother and a sister, and his parents, who are both still alive. Gianni tells me how, together, they often had to take care of his mother, who suffered from repeated episodes of depression that arose after a road accident in which she was hit by a car as she was walking along.

A year before coming to me, Gianni had been working abroad, where some colleagues had involved him in an experience with prostitutes. He had not taken part in any "kinky sex", but in any case part of him "had said I shouldn't", but he had not managed to resist.

Since then, he had begun to feel increasingly worse. At home, he had even tried to commit suicide, putting a plastic bag over his head. Saved by his girlfriend, he had spent a few days in hospital, during which time "I had lost every notion of time and space; I felt like an idiot."

When he comes to me he is clearly in a state of agitation, depressed, and with persecutory peaks. He stammers and his legs twitch constantly; he is frenetic and full of anxiety.

Nevertheless, along with wanting relief from his great suffering, he also really wants to understand and to work with me, which I feel is genuine and sincere. So we begin an analysis that, after an initial period, settles down to three sessions a week.

At first, I follow him closely, functioning transferentially as a mother who tries to propose energy and holding, as opposed to the death of the emotional experience. In fact, at times, he becomes almost disorientated, his thought fragmented and detached, incoherent, and illogical.

My voice seems to me at times to be a sound from within that holds steady and attempts to offer equilibrium.

It becomes increasingly clear how important it is to work with Gianni by bringing to centre stage a robust countertransferential listening, even more so than with other patients, because he is unable to pick up the game of relaunching verbal exchange.

When I intervene, he sometimes feels hostility; yet I "mysteriously" sense that he is a person with sufficient energy to be able to enter into this experience and continue it.

After several months, a phase of greater elaboration begins. He also begins to say that "he is thinking about indefinite things", and I feel that this might hint at the drafting of an idea.

Gradually, persecutory and threatening dreams appear: dreams with evil beings that are transformed into young children, then into sweaters, which he has to burn, or into threads wound up like electric wires, balls of wires, piled up in his garage. In others, a giant larva and a butterfly emerge from behind a skirting board; he manages to kill them: they were the source of the strange sensations that he had felt after his brother had given him books containing pseudo-religious images. Or he dreams that he is spitting out golden crucifixes. He manages to get the better of this, but it is difficult and he is very afraid. A man takes his hands, which peel, and then he sees his feet crawling with ants. At the same time, feelings of jealousy towards his brother emerge very clearly.

It is difficult to understand what is persecuting him because his anxiety reveals very little, whereas he often attempts a personal "do-it-yourself" working-through in an effort to find compensation and eliminate opportunities for new crises. He also brings dreams in which he is with many others and he has to reach a graveyard.

I cannot quite understand what is being prepared inside him and between us, but I perceive that these movements are harbingers of something that has to reveal itself in the analytic relationship.

At this point, one day he recounts this dream:

> Alone at home I'm watching a film on my PC. The characters were behaving like those in the museum dream, in the dangerous

game ... The film was also interacting with me. The characters were coming into the room, they were doing things and I was frightened. I had to watch this film again so that these people would not do certain things [felt by him to be negative]. Watching it again, I manage to catch some details that allow me to finish watching it without problems, that is, preventing the characters from coming into the room ...

He then speaks of peeing as an act equal to eliminating toxins, and then that he does not know if he can succeed in handling these characters or whether, instead, he does not feel like facing them, and so he directs them again in their film.

This dream takes up the events in the "museum dream" of a few sessions previously, in which a game to be played in a museum was dominated by the presence of some aspects and characters that could become "diabolical".

I tell him that I believe an important point is that he is frightened by the dream, because the characters come so close, they come right in with us here, as I have mentioned on many occasions, but he is afraid that they are diabolical; he must keep them at bay, impose some limits. I feel that this time he is moving to a decidedly deeper, and also riskier—for him—level where there are aspects that he feels are very dangerous. So it is necessary to keep them at bay: if they are too close they are uncomfortable, frightening. If he puts them back in the film, it is as though he is trying to make them more something of the imagination, thus avoiding their becoming concrete, which is terrifying for him.

From that moment on, the form/dream of the computer with characters that come out of it is repeated many times, in various declensions of the story. So, the characters from the screen have to be welcomed into the room, and these, from one time to the next, bring hate, competitiveness, jealousy, rivalry, and dysmorphic-phobic anxieties. Dreams occur containing the gravestones of husband, wife, and son from which skeletons emerge, mother-like "good people" who are the subject of a television programme, fathers who first smash shop windows with terrible blows and then try to shoot him, although he is protected by "a friend", or there is the grandmother who prevents him from turning off the television, "otherwise the whole circuit won't work". There is something heavy and morbidly psychotic in this material; however, he tells me that he feels growing trust that he will not be thrown away if he reveals it all here.

More time passes and the "chaos" seems to take further shape and organisation: Gianni tells me these two dreams that seem to me to represent a further, significant change in the relationship in general, and also in the way that the patient and I can relate to that particular digital world that the analysis has brought to centre stage:

> I tell a work colleague that I can leave straightaway, but the problem will be for him to find another like me. A young woman was helping me with the computer: "Here you have to click on this button and open the programme in this other way." The software was the same though.

There are many aspects in Gianni's analytic profile that have struck me and led me to further thoughts and reflections about the relationship with the world of informatics. First of all, the presence of this unusual "inversion in the flow" shown by Gianni in using digital and media space in general compared to what is more common—in some way retrieving the characters projected inside that dimension—has often brought to my mind two films by David Cronenberg, *Videodrome* and *eXistenZ*.

In *Videodrome*, a dangerous television signal produces tumorous modifications of the brain, which cause hallucinations, among which that of seeing something come out of a screen, deforming it and transforming it into a fusion between technology and human being.

In *eXistenZ*, one witnesses a progressive isomorphism between external reality and virtual reality, represented here as totally immersive.

Gianni shows me the progressive overflowing of internal characters within a space that is both inside the analytic field where the relationship between us is brought to life, and outside a virtual/mental space that can no longer keep them imprisoned.

This space (which in its turn, like a Möbius strip, is at the same time and for many reasons internal and external) is evidently not the space of shared social reality, but that of the dream. These characters succeed in returning inside this dimension, allowing the conditions for the development over time of an aggregation in the form of meaning. These aggregations, if they were really to overflow into factual reality and become concrete and sensorially perceptible, would be pandemically hallucinatory. In this case, we would witness the path of the not-worked-through objects/characters in the opposite direction to that of normal perception, that is, in the visual retrieval of things that have first been evacuated, expelled into the space of external reality, as Bion, too, suggests.

Instead, in this case, the space of the dream, not daily reality and not even evacuative VR, is the first containing box; the dream space takes on the nature of container, revealer, and communicator of this dynamic need within the patient.

The figures which progressively present themselves to us are not, therefore, expelled, unmetabolised, but remain in the dream space, in a psychic, virtual space, understood as potential and potentially usable for subsequent elaboration. We are called on to tolerate the fact that a world felt as frightening and destructive might overflow into our space, with the risk of our being colonised by its madness. If the characters rage uncontrollably, in place of real manifestations of presences, this may result in haemorrhage and madness, and everything would be lost and Gianni risks remaining empty and mad. On the one hand, the erupting avalanche of characters, sweeping him (and us) away, will render him forever lost in the universe of a desperate madness; on the other hand, in doing this, he will remain completely emptied of his entire self.

Getting the characters to come into the (analytic) room therefore requires a giant leap of trust. By the way this is a condition that we can define variously in terms of psychoanalytic models: we could discuss this later.

So, the characters (and the undigested facts that give them substance) have taken on the characteristics of shattered objects, which, however, have attempted to return by passing through the video by way of dreams and the conjoined "ferrying" force of myself and the patient. They succeed in returning to demand sufficient space and time, volume and colour, with no dazzling by the blinding light of delusion and hallucination (Resnik, 1986). They ask to be heard, to be present; perhaps they even want to play, like the characters in the *Purple Rose of Cairo* (Allen, 1985), though always within a capacity for working-through that only in analysis, in the field of analysis, finds energy and realisation.

I believe that the space in the dream can be further thought of as the virtual/oneiric space (true intermediate space) of his mind at work with mine in the session, a genuine internal and field space in which we can semantically and mentally make the virtual coincide with the oneiric. The patient does it: the characters come out of the screen but come into the working-through dream space, where they receive a vital push that they had not had until then.

The space of the analytic field so formed, in the profound immersion of the two minds at work, provides an opposing dimension to the mad infinity into which the patient was terrified of falling.

When, after much time, he brings the dream in which he is in charge of, and works, the computer, and, therefore, is able to enter by himself in some way, another important movement becomes clear. Going into the computer is comparable to going into his own mind. At the beginning, it was necessary to get all the characters to go inside whatever could be identified variously as my mind/space of the analytic room. Now Gianni can see them and visit them better by himself, and I take on the function of giving him just a "few indications", like a mother who is no longer asked for total constant attention and care. He is beginning to know the source code and manage it, to give to its virtual space the potential for a more vital development, where he can hope that, as Winnicott tells us, a true experience of living, rather than simply functioning, may come to life.

References

Allen, W. (1985). *The Purple Rose of Cairo* (film). USA: Orion Pictures.
Bonaminio, V., Gabbard, G., & Moreno, J. (2010). Panel: Psychoanalysis and Virtuality. 46th IPA Congress, 31 July 2009, Chicago. *International Journal of Psychoanalysis*, 91: 985–988.
Cronenberg, D. (Dir.) (1983). *Videodrome* (film). Universal Pictures.
Cronenberg, D. (Dir.) (1999). *eXistenZ* (film). Alliance Atlantics (Canada) & Momentum Pictures (UK).
Eigen, M., & Malater, E. (2007). Special issue on the Internet. *Psychoanalytic Review*, 94(1): 99–139.
Hautmann, G. (1999). Immaginazione e interpretazione [Imagination and interpretation]. In: *La psicoanalisi tra arte e biologia* [*Psychoanalysis between Art and Biology*]. Rome: Borla.

Marzi, A. (Ed.) (2013). *Psicoanalisi, Identità e Internet. Esplorazioni nel cyberspace* [*Psychoanalysis, Identity and the Internet: Cyberspace Explorations*]. Milan: Franco Angeli.

Marzi, A. (Ed.) (2016). *Psychoanalysis, Identity and the Internet: Explorations into Cyberspace*. London: Karnac.

Resnik, S. (1986). *L'esperienza delirante* [*The Delusional Experience*]. Torino: Bollati Boringhieri.

Sixth British–Italian Dialogue (2011). *Dream Space and Virtual Space in the Analytic Process*. London: British Psychoanalytical Society.

Suarez, J. C., & Jasso, E. N. (2002). El impacto de nuevas técnicas y nuevas 'realidades' en psicoanálisis [The impact of new technologies and new realities in psychoanalysis]. *The International Journal of Psychoanalysis, 83*(4): 926–930.

CHAPTER 5

Contemporary hysterical body

Fernando Orduz

Introduction by João Seabra Diniz

Fernando Orduz, a Colombian psychoanalyst, visited Lisbon to participate in the national colloquium on sexuality in 2017. At the time he was the president of FEPAL, and his ease of communication, spontaneity, and ability to engage listeners was remarkable. This is the text that underpinned his lecture: about the hysterical body.

Of course, changes in the evolution of knowledge and cultural organisation, linked to new possibilities offered by various types of progress, lead to new conceptions of man and his way of functioning. The author focuses on the field of medicine and talks about the evolution of Freud's conceptions and how they can be understood today. The titles he gives to his chapter make very clear the route he intends to take his presentation and the ideas he is to present.

The content of the general title is developed into two parts, which are: "Prologuising history" and "Contemporary Dora".

In Ancient Greece, medicine "was the art of reading the body". In Freud's first case studies, "emphasis was given to the body as a communication system". And focusing on this dynamic, Freud analyses a set of forces that place the body "in a continuous state of becoming".

Medicine, and culture in general, have dealt with this problem over time, trying to understand its messages. Freud and Goethe both looked at the problem. To illustrate this point, the author quotes a sentence by Freud in his speech at the ceremony of his acceptance of the Goethe Prize.

In his connection with history, Plato's name is not forgotten either.

And the author asks how Dora, who was Freud's client, that is, contemporary Dora, would express herself today in the face of the enormous differences that exist in our society.

At the end of his chapter, he gives the answer. "Hysteria continues to stream through the body, but not only through a painful body ... but through a body that enjoys and amuses itself ..."

* * *

Prologuising history

Freud's psychoanalytic discovery is in some ways tied to corporal manifestations. Such manifestations present themselves as a written text to be read by Freud as the body expressing a contradiction between a patient's painful moaning and its anatomo-pathological counterpart.

I highlight the term corporal manifestation because Freud was a neurophysiologist, not a psychiatrist. As any other nineteenth-century physician, he was a symptom reader, a sign hunter. Objective signals called signs or subjective signals called symptoms are the body's surfacing reflections of internal organs that suffered some type of damage, failure, or alteration. The skin, δέρμᾰ, is a blank page where illnesses leave marks. Let's think of jaundice, petechiae, skin eruptions, all of them surfacing effects of internal processes occurring inside the body.

Ancient Greek medicine was the art of reading the body, conjectural and speculative. Preceding Hippocrates, Alcméon of Croton was perhaps the first to gather random observations from previous generations, speculatively organising a causal order by proposing active principles (dynamics) to explain observable phenomena. Such causal factors were related to principles as cold, heat, humidity, dryness. He attributes the origin of disease to any of these qualities' supremacy (μοναρχία— *monarchia*), as opposed to the equilibrium among them, health.

From Ancient Greece to the nineteenth century, the speculative physician trained his eyes to master perception of details. This allowed a delicate, meticulous, and fine observation of the body's appearance, in order to inductively speculate the cause. The Ancient physician was a cartographer, an ambiance reader, reading further than the patient's body. Rather than the mere body, he would have studied the city public space, the water system, the wind currents, and the sunrise.

Medicine's practice based in semiology (reading of signs and symptoms) had the role of examining the body by observing, touching, smelling, hearing it, sensible experience which, along with logical reflection integrate the art of healing a patient's ailment.

In all of Freud's early study cases, emphasis was given to the body as a communication system:

> Emmy spoke in a low voice as though with difficulty and her speech was from time to time subject to spastic interruption amounting to a stammer. There were frequent convulsive tic-like movements of her face and the muscles of her neck, during which some of them, specially the right sterno-cleido-mastoid, stood out prominently.
>
> Lucy had entirely lost her sense of smell and was almost continuously pursued by one or two subjective olfactory sensations.
>
> Adolescent Dora was suffering from a cough and hoarseness.
>
> Elisabeth complains of hyperalgesia of the skin and muscles (inner right thigh). Observing from a distance, Freud observes how she enters the room with a very particular way of walking and standing (*stehen*). She complains of pain when walking and walks with the upper part of her body bent forward, without the use of any support and without any recognised pathological trace.

As mentioned before, Freud does not read simply the body's signs or symptoms. For instance, departing from the German word *stehen* (meaning both standing and being), he connects Elisabeth's body and story. She was standing when the father had his first cardiac arrest. She was also standing beside her dead sister's bed. Her body is standing facing death. Freud links body and soul, the remaining pain a loss, after death, which migrates to the body, it gets somatised.

Elisabeth was left alone, without a father and sister, without love. She was grieving about being lonely (*stehen*). She couldn't step forward with her purpose, she was standing (*stehen*). That was the symbolic meaning of her aphasia. A verbal expression of not being able to step forward derived from her body's inhibited action.

Freud gradually discovers that behind Elisabeth's ailment is an act that marked her body. Taking care of her father, resting his leg on the inner right thigh while renewing bandages, left a reminder, a bodily feeling tying further corporal symptoms by extension or opposition.

Freud stated that walking, standing, sitting, and lying are actions connected with functions and of situations—the painful areas in Elisabeth's body—the legs. The body feeling experienced when caring for her father is a somatic remain, dissociated from her own story but alive on the body surface.

Pain is a symptom. It is subjective nor objective. From Elisabeth's case, Freud discovers that when he approaches a memory node, physical pain heightens, leading him to think about a conversion from psychic excitation to corporal pain. Ultimately, he is showing us how behind a narrative wrapping, a fantasy wrapping, lies a body (an area of the body) sustaining and triggering a specific discursiveness.

Freud allows us to glimpse a hysterical body operating as a language. As a narrative of a story from the past surfacing in the present through body memories, gestures, footprints, traces. As opposed to Charcot's iconic image of the body where the prominence of a visual spectacle has prevalence, this is a body where the act of writing is predominant.

Whether a story is incarnated in words or not, it writes itself on the body and transfers to it. Time seems to be a burin. Body, the cooper plate where traces are engraved. Charcot believed hysteria exists as a visible spectacle, which cannot be heard. Their female bodies were exhibited in an auditorium, much like a theatre, for an audience eager to witness the appearance of a corporeal symptom. Surprised eyes, amazed gazes, vivid exclamations from the public. Hysteria has always fabricated visibility scenarios, we have seen it and been shaken up by it, but its words are always disguised behind the visual spectacle.

The French psychiatrist, a product of his time, was obsessed by physical measurements, quantifying an ecstatic body. Such a body is not only shaped as a measurable surface, but also holds the Industrial Revolution and Modernity's footprints inscribed on it: the importance of unveiling that which is hidden. A body that is more image than real presence, more visual than tactile, more mirror-like or photographic than performative, more iconophilic than iconoclast.

Charcot's hysteria revealed to Freud the *mise en scène* of a body's dramatisation. The nineteenth-century female body depicts actions beyond its own conscious intentions. Two centuries before, in Salem, it was presumed that such a female body was possessed by the devil. A question unfolding from these facts, and which will remain unanswered here, would be what the female body possesses which, along the centuries, keeps interrogating the knowledge through all times.

Freud opens a different dimension from Charcot's visual modernity. He discovers a body animated by vital forces, breaking the univocal image of the photographic body. Thus, challenging the identity of such a univocal body image, whether surface or volume, he uncovers a flux of forces which puts the body in a continuous state of becoming, possessed by demons different from those animating the haunted Salem bodies. For psychoanalysis, the alienated body of the hysteric exposed or reflected an intention. Freud addresses such intention more as a playful demon, a pulsion (compulsion, repulsion, expulsion, impulsion) rather than as a religious Catholic demon. A libidinal form that takes different forms depending on where it surfaces in the human body: oral devouring love, tactile controller, distant visual, deeply olfactory.

The idea of a corporeality as a force and/or action has been present from the origins of Western thought. In Greece, around the times of Homer, there was no word meaning a body, a unity. The closest to it was the word *sôma* (σῶμα), which appears on the *Iliad*, to designate a corpse, a body lacking movement or vital force. The idea of unity is built over a dead body. It is rather peculiar how Western medicine still builds and reproduces its knowledge over a dead body lying on a cold stone.

The unity provided by a mortuary image led Egypt to corpse embalming, so they would endure forever. That is why the corpse wore a mask, an object representing it for eternity. Let's remember that the Latin word *persona* means the mask worn by an actor. It is that which we carry in front of others to obtain a univocal image. This is what plastic surgery and juvenile suicides advocate: to preserve the image of eternal youth against the decay of the passage of time.

Within the twentieth-century French tradition, from Wallon to Lacan, the West constructed yet another univocal meaning based on the mirror image of the body. According to a school of thought with regards to the psyche, children take a long time to be aware of their bodies. For several months they have nothing but plural and fragmented perceptions from the body, a chaotic experience that becomes unitary in the face of the mirror image reflection. A unitary experience that occurs on the other side of the mirror, in a virtual, imaginary space, contrasting the visible body (unitary) to the sensitive body (fragmentary).

These concepts are associated with Nietzsche's ideas of the Dionysian and the Apollonian. Dionysus as a shapeless force trapped in Apollo's illusory form, which is just imaginary. The Apollonian representation is pleasing because it gives form, while the emergence of the Dionysian impulse is disturbing. The impression of a fragmentary Dionysian form allows Freud's perverse polymorphous idea. In Greece, the living body representation is closer to the idea of a polymorphous force than to the *sôma* unitary concept, which refers to a dead body.

In "Instincts and their vicissitudes" Freud says:

> By the pressure [*Drang*] of an instinct we understand its motor factor, the amount of force or the measure of the demand for work which it represents. The characteristic of exercising pressure is common to all instincts; it is in fact their very essence. (Freud, 1915c, p. 122)

Drang, the essence of instincts, is also the concept that drives the German Romantic Spirit. In the acceptance speech of the Goethe Prize, given at his Frankfurt home in 1930, Freud sustains that:

> Goethe always respected Eros, never tried to belittle his power, he followed his primitive or even mischievous exteriorisations with

no less attention than his extreme sublimations. And, it seems to me, he did not maintained less decisively than Plato, in an earlier age, its essential unity through all kind of manifestations. (Freud, 1930e)

For Goethe the principle of the Word as the principle of life was unfeasible. In reality, the fundamental principle for this movement should not be sought in a transcendent world … this principle must be expressed in terms of force and action. In Faust it says: "In the beginning was force [*Kraft*] … In the beginning was action".

Drang unleashes passion force (*Kraft*), which if taking a stormy (*Sturm*) form will overwhelm any attempt of containment by limits, at any time.

Contemporary Dora

If Dora came to our practice, how would she express to us her suffering? Most likely not through the ailment of the body that is paralysed or loses mobility. In today's culture, numbness and motor paralysis are no longer the forms of expression of the body, rather the opposite. Today, the body is hyper-stimulated and hyper-motorised. Modern life has become a permanent stimulator of our senses and a driving force in opposition to stillness. We are sensitive and hyper-kinetic, stressed and in ongoing action. Now, it is about the acting body, showing itself, evidencing itself no longer within the passivity of being looked at, but in the activity to be looked at.

Hysteria always had an epidermal character, meaning that it is a disorder or pathology with surfacing manifestations. Today it remains a structure presenting manifestations in the *sôma*. Have we stopped encountering hysterical behaviours in favour of emergent narcissistic pathologies? Or is it simply that due to its own structure, hysteria exists before our eyes, without being identified? Do we disguise it under the so-called new pathologies?

On account of its building mechanisms: imitation, suggestion, and identification, the hysterical symptom is currently masked in new forms of expression on the visible surface of the body. Perhaps it exists despite our unawareness.

Freud's early theories on hysteria were concerned with formulating economic explanations: a power surge that overloads the system and cannot find a somatic bypass, therefore seeking paths through the *sôma*. An obstacle that prevents potential energy from being released and therefore manifests somatically. The hysterical body used to become paralysed or anesthetised as a result of a sexuality or an energy that was detonated, being contained later on with no other possibility of emerging. Surely, paralysis and anaesthesia spoke of what has happened to them, about a paralysed energy, leaving a feeling that, since it was not an act, it was a mark of insensitivity.

Aiming to preserve Freud's explanatory tradition, what can we say today about hysteria, under the concepts of hyper-kinesis and hyper-stimulation? An unanalysed energy, finding multiple ways to express itself. If the body is an expression of it, then it could be thought that the hysterical body today gets agitated and overexcited in spaces of permanent visibility, in a modern version of Charcot's theatres of which we have spoken before.

Trained as psychoanalysts, we have repeatedly heard since the beginning the idea that modern pathologies have changed. We have turned from neuroses towards borderline pathologies. I do not doubt that pathologies can disappear from the face of the earth, and in fact the presence of vaccines in the history of humanity has shown this as fact.

But has psychoanalysis operated like a vaccine on the mind? Has its theory of repression led to a social conscience aware of how its own defences work, driving to dilute disease from the face of the consulting rooms and of the political classifications of mental health?

It is important to rethink hysteria, the structural body of our analytical endeavours and the cornerstone for the analyst–patient relationship. Recognition of suggestibility within the hysterical existence is a historical fact. Also pointed out by psychoanalysis, its symptoms vary according to the fashion and trends of the cosmos.

In contemporary times, the hysterical body quivers in a different fashion, now in theatres under a changed label: "gym". It becomes hyper-sensitised in the "spa". It is dramatised in any place that provides scenarios: the TV, the street, the office, and meetings. Embodied hysteria screams today at concerts or in a doctor's consulting room. Hyper-stimulation is symbolised by the cry, which links with pain. Somehow the painful complaint (or the orgasmic scream) continues to attend our practices, it goes through the doctor's offices, keeps trying to talk to the doctor who, by not listening to it, makes today's hysteria seek the consultation of alternative medicines.

Hysteria today continues to stream through the body, but not only through a painful body and its numerous complaints (fibromyalgia, osteoarthritis, headaches), but through a body that enjoys and amuses itself. It puts on make-up, tattoos, pierces itself, combs its hair, dresses up, and undergoes surgery. And it suffers endlessly by not achieving that body image that it craves.

References

Freud, S. (1915c). Instincts and their vicissitudes. *S. E.*, *14*: 109–140. London: Hogarth.

Freud, S. (1930e). Address delivered in the Goethe House at Frankfurt. *S. E.*, *21*: 208. London: Hogarth.

CHAPTER 6

Connecting the International Psychoanalytical Association to our psychoanalytical community

Sergio Eduardo Nick

Introduction by Rui Aragão Oliveira

The decade 2010 to 2020 was marked by a continuous effort of restructuring and growth in the Portuguese Psychoanalytical Society, after an episode of a deep institutional crisis. Several boards were involved, with the collaboration of many members who dedicated themselves in a frank and intense effort to the defence of psychoanalytical knowledge.

They have been able to draw on the experience and support of the International Psychoanalytical Association (IPA), in a regular dialogue which has mobilised several colleagues such as Charles Handly, Paul Denis, Rosina Perelberg, and, in particular, Stefano Bolognini and Marilia Eisenstein.

When Virginia Ungar and Sergio Nick took over the IPA board, we felt it was important to express the importance of their presence to psychoanalysts, and how significant it would be to promote greater proximity to members.

Sergio Nick, in an act of great generosity, a characteristic that is clear to see, immediately offered to pay a visit in 2018, where he had the opportunity to share his clinical reflections, and also to offer us a unique presentation on the stature and influence of the IPA today, both in its scientific and human scope.

This chapter essentially sets out the presentation he shared with his Portuguese colleagues, holding psychoanalysis as the guardian of humanism, respect, and dignity, and where the IPA is a funda-mental historical legacy for the identity, training, and defence of all psychoanalysts, in a multiplicity of tasks and scope that we are cer-tain dignifies the legacy of Sigmund Freud. We can see not only the evolution of IPA's aims, but also the complexity of its organisation today.

It is refreshing to note the immensity of functions that this global organisation now offers its members: in its basic and ongoing train-ing, for scientific debate, and for the serious and organised presence of psychoanalytical thinking in the main international forums for political action, whether in the social, health, educational, or cultural fields.

His lecture was crucial for a substantial change in the relationship that many colleagues have been building with IPA, starting to rec-ognise the institution as a stimulating and creative reference for the development of identity as a psychoanalyst.

* * *

Psychoanalysis and its characteristics
(from Freud to his followers)

I believe that psychoanalysis will continue to exist as long as there is humanism. I refer to the humane aspects described by Freud such as helplessness, distress, uncertainty, amongst others. Likewise, his followers worked on various humane aspects such as loss, attachment, object relations, affections, loneliness, guilt, resentment, anger, amongst many other humane elements. In my view, humanism would be the *sine qua non* condition for the psychoanalyst and the *raison d'être* of psychoanalysis today. In this sense, psychoanalysis would be a guardian of humanism as it seeks to highlight, for each subject, the importance of their experiences, feelings, memories, and inheritances. In this line of thinking, we could oppose psychoanalysis to the scientific movement that aims to see men as a machine or as a result of purely biological processes.

When talking about the values at the core of his psychoanalytic practice, Ogden (2005) emphasises the analyst's need to "be humane", that is, the principle that he treats his patient "and all those his patient's life impinges upon—in a humane way, in a way that at all times honors human dignity" (Ogden, 2005, p. 19). But what would it be like to treat the patient humanely? The author will say that the meaning of "being humane" in the psychoanalytic setting is more easily exemplified by its violation than by its effectiveness. To illustrate, he gives us some examples such as when an analyst treats the patient's psychological illness with neglect when opening his emails during the session, or if the analyst exempts himself from some intervention, continuing with the "analysis as usual" (Ogden, 2005, p. 20) when faced with a situation of inhumanity on the part of the patient (to himself, to the analyst, or to others). For Ogden (2005) under such circumstances, it is incumbent upon the analyst not to cease being a psychoanalyst, but to become a psychoanalyst doing something else (Ogden, 2005, p. 20; Winnicott, 1962).

On the other hand, we are now faced with hyper-connectivity and excess of information which is, in a way, shifting us away from the human or, at least, introducing us to another way of relating to it. In this way, we must try to think how the human will present itself in the virtual world. As an example, in the past, when posting some content, there were four, five, or even ten friends either saying: "I liked what you said/posted!" or giving it a *like*. However, those who posted knew where these likes came from. Nowadays, differently, when we see a person who calls her/himself a *digital influencer*, we assume that what seems to matter to her/him is not the face or the human behind the *like*, but the numbers: the greater the number of followers, the greater their importance in today's world. By conveying messages on a large scale, one ends up losing its intimate aspect, to access a question of universality and uniformity of what is transmitted, in the sectarian sense of the term.

When conceiving psychoanalysis as a bastion of the human, we get closer to writers, poets, and novelists. However, we will find an important distinction: we psychoanalysts, unlike them, when thinking about these issues within the humanist perspective, we do it from a discourse that is idiosyncratic. Psychoanalysis will always take into account the different factors of influence and relationships that each subject suffers, either with their ancestors or in their psychic development (and with that I refer to everything that constitutes psyche, such as identifications and defences). Furthermore, by locating the subject's truth in the unconscious, psychoanalysis operates a displacement of the subject from the fields of the *ego* and consciousness towards the domains of drive and otherness (Birman, 1998). As we all know, Freud places psychoanalysis as the third major narcissistic wound in the history of mankind (the others having been produced by Copernicus and Darwin), "which is endeavoring to prove to the ego of each one of us that he is not even master in his own house" (Freud, 1916–1917).

The IPA, therefore, has a relevant role not only in promoting the development of psychoanalysis, but in its corollary, the defence of humanism.

The IPA

Talking about the IPA is always an enchanting task. It is an association that, after several years of institutional work, matters a lot to me. Like a son to whom one has dedicated himself for years, the IPA ended up being a space to think not only about psychoanalysis but also to sow its future.

When I started institutional work, many spoke of a "psychoanalytic crisis". It took me some time to understand that a crisis demands not only racing for its rescue, but an opportunity to develop a practice and a thinking that has been going on for more than 100 years since its birth. According to what I heard recently, we should never waste a crisis!

Getting to know our international association means to get in touch with a complex organism, which therefore houses many aspects that interpenetrate and have an effect on each other. Few know the IPA as it really is. On the one hand, being an IPA psychoanalyst means for many feeling of belonging to a select group, with a tradition that dates back to the beginnings of psychoanalysis and its creator—Sigmund Freud—and with a vast set of knowledge and history. However, on the other hand, it is a long, arduous, and exhausting journey. Psychoanalytic training in "IPA standards", is one of the most rigorous, if not the most; both in terms of time and dedication to the famous "tripod" of training: personal analysis, supervision of clinical cases, and clinical and theoretical seminars.

As an institution, the IPA is much more than I just described, and this chapter seeks to show the public a little of what I got to know about it.

The current IPA organisation (2020)

We define the IPA as a membership organisation—it exists because of its members, and for their benefit. The IPA is the world's primary accrediting and regulatory body for the psychoanalytic profession. Differently from other institutions, the IPA is constituted by its members. They have the right to vote and to have their representatives voting for them.

Its primary aims are to foster and enhance members' sense of participation in and belonging to an international psychoanalytic organisation and community. Also, it intends to advance psychoanalysis and to ensure the continued vigour and development of the science of psychoanalysis.

As a motto for our administration (Virginia Ungar, IPA president; Sergio Nick, IPA vice-president, 2017–2021), we chose "One IPA For All". With this, we wanted to convey the idea of a greater presence in the lives of members, in contrast to the super-egoic and normative aspect that previously caused so much distance between the association and its members. After all, if the IPA has survived so many crises, something strong unites us. One can think of the aspects linked to the honourable heritage of it having been created by Freud, but also by the many illustrious psychoanalysts who contributed so much to the development of psychoanalytic theory and practice.

The IPA is currently composed of 12,783 members, 5,199 candidates, 85 societies, one regional association, and 14 study groups in 47 countries across the world.[1] As for its overall structure, the IPA is divided into administrative and governance committees, scientific committees, development committees and the IPA in the community committees.

The IPA Board of Representatives consists of three officers (president, vice-president, and treasurer), plus seven representatives from each

---

[1] Latest release on 13 August 2020.

of the IPA regions (Europe, North America, Latin America). We have recently added one Asia-Pacific representative that has an observer role. The Board adopts and modifies IPA criteria and establishes rules, procedures, and policies for its, and the IPA's, operations, all of which must be consistent with these rules, and any binding resolutions adopted by IPA members.[2] The executive committee is composed of the officers and three regional representatives (one from each region).

What the IPA offers its members

To answer the question so often asked, we can list some bodies and actions already available:

- Biennial Congress, the largest psychoanalytic congress in the world
- an opportunity to be part of the world's most international and theoretically diverse psychoanalytic organisation
- sponsorship and development of about thirty-five new groups around the world, including in many places where analysis has never existed before
- the IPA *Inter-Regional Encyclopedic Dictionary of Psychoanalysis*, a unique reference work produced by teams of analysts from all IPA regions
- the eJournal *Psychoanalysis.today* (a joint initiative between IPA and the regional organisations EPF, FEPAL, NAPsaC+APsaA)
- the CAPSA inter-regional travel fund, allowing analysts from one IPA region to present, supervise, and teach in another region
- a US$1m loan programme to help candidates with the costs of training
- research: over 450 research projects funded over the past twenty years, with results available on the IPA website
- around fifty committees, task forces and advisory groups, with around 600 members, on a wide range of vital topics
- library of policy and best practice documents (e.g., policy on ethics, confidentiality, etc.)

---

[2] Taken from the IPA's Procedural Code document 'Role of the Board of Representatives and link Responsibilities'.

- partnership with Routledge, for a book publication programme via the IPA publications committee
- a diverse array of awards to recognise IPA members who have made outstanding contributions to psychoanalysis
- online archive of IPA historical documents and IPA Congress presentations (under development)
- access to Lexicon, our offices in central London, with expert staff providing advice and assistance to members
- the IPA website, with access to information and services, the online roster of nearly 13,000 members, webinars, and online debates
- webinars: provides IPA members, candidates, and the general public an opportunity to hear from acclaimed psychoanalysts discussing a variety of topics
- IPA blog: a space for the IPA to maintain a commentary on social, cultural, and political issues from a psychoanalytic perspective
- Social media committee: more than 33,000 people follow the IPA on *Facebook*, which is also active on *Twitter*, *YouTube*, and *Instagram*— a vital importance to our strategy for member engagement and outreach
- Visiting candidates programme: a collaborative initiative between the IPA and IPSO that funds candidate's visits to institutes in a different region
- IPA in the Community committees: a new structure of committees created at the start of our administration with the purpose of increasing IPA psychoanalysis' presence in the community. The IPA in the Community committee sub-areas are: health (both general medicine and mental health), education (across all age groups), culture, violence, law, and humanitarian organisations
- IPA podcasts: actually divided into two categories—IPA in health and IPA podcasts.

Such a list shows how large and complex the IPA is, with members usually taking direct advantage of only some of these possibilities. On the other hand, they are indirectly affected by many of these different bodies and actions.

Anyway, one of the biggest challenges to an international association like ours is to show members what we are doing. Some will always see

IPA as a distant and unvalued body. It is our duty to tie us all together, and to promote psychoanalysis. It also brings the question of "why should I pay the IPA dues?" As stated in a letter by Arthur Leonoff, a Canadian psychoanalyst and member of the IPA's task force on representation:

> No IPA and there will be no psychoanalysis, at least as we know it. There will be no international dialogue, no new groups, no over-arching identity and source of ethics. We will be truly local and, in the short term, saving money until the very local organisations have to replace what the IPA does and then inevitably raise their dues … It is the best money we spend when it comes to psychoanalysis. The IPA has our back and backs us up in every respect. It is us and we are it. Without the IPA, strong and vital, psychoanalysis will wither … We might do okay with less local and more international but the converse is not true. There is good reason why psychoanalysis never retracted into a series of local entities. It is an international discipline with a central organisa-tion that gives meaning to the rest. This is essential and needs careful nurturing and management.

The IPA during the Covid-19 pandemic

During the new coronavirus pandemic (in 2020), we sought to quickly implement actions that could mitigate what we considered urgent, both for the institution and for its members. You can find a list below where the actions shown demonstrate how we can deliver, in a contemporary world, a helpful and comprehensive association to its members:

- We decided to suspend, until further notice, the requirement for IPA component societies to consult the education committee before using remote training analysis and supervision (as stated by the procedural code).
- We asked the board for approval to postpone the increase on dues planned for 2021.
- We are currently having several exchanges with component societies regarding dues and humanitarian matters.

- We asked the social media and confidentiality committees to organise a document with guidelines for telehealth.
- We launched the IPA Health Crisis Listserv for the Covid-19 pandemic, organised by the IPA in health committee. In order to provide a space for our members and candidates to exchange experiences, concerns, and reflections, and to support each other.
- The Listserv has 1,200 subscribers and, up to now, there are over 750 contributions in different languages.
- We set up the Covid-19 resource page "Stay Connected" on the IPA website with over 70 articles, papers, and other useful materials in different languages.
- We organised the Covid-19 special series of webinars. We decided to increase the frequency of webinars: since the end of March up to August 2020 there have been plenty of webinars in different languages, including: English, Spanish, French, German, Italian, and Portuguese. We also doubled the capacity of attendees.
- We organised special editions of the two IPA podcasts "IPA on and off the couch" and "IPA talks on psychoanalysis", dedicated to the current pandemic.
- We decided to postpone the Asia Pacific Sydney Conference to 2024. We are closely supervising the Vancouver Congress contracts evaluating the possibility of a hybrid event.
- We decided to cancel the in-person Rio de Janeiro board meeting and organised an online meeting.
- The IPA climate committee produced the video "Corona, climate and grandma".
- Finally, we are very proud to share the initiatives of many of our IPA component societies all around the world, that are offering free online assistance and forums to their communities. Additionally, we have plenty of different work made by our committees that wouldn't fit this space.

The definition of contemporary is existing at the same time or existing at the present time period. If we aim to be a contemporary organisation, it is fundamental that we build a way for our members and others interested in psychoanalysis to keep in touch with our actions, participating, exchanging, and therefore maintaining our organisation in order to stay alive. As an example, the first eight Covid-19 webinars were seen by more than 21,000 people, from 108 different countries. This shows how this "new world" can facilitate communication with many places which we barely could have thought of before. The ListServe, whilst having about 750 contributions, is another example of how to connect members to each other, to share doubts, thoughts, and affections. As an international organisation, we seek to get members' interactions in a more fluid and interregional way. In order to accompany a specific period of time concerning interregional and intercultural aspects, the IPA must be able to hear its members, its differences, and to present solutions that complies with its complexities.

Psychoanalysis after the Covid-19 pandemic

There are many unforeseen paths to us after the new coronavirus pandemic, including the fact we will be in a favourable professional field if we are able to convey our capacity to deal with the emergence of trauma, anguish, and depression that will follow it. Mental health issues are at the core of media news and comments as have never been before. The awareness of a psychic life, both in a good and a bad sense, has come to light. Social isolation and the need to get together at home led people to reflect on their relationships, affections, and embodied co-presence.

As seen by many psychoanalysts, hidden conflicts have arisen, with an appeal for help to families, couples, and children, as well as to individuals. We psychoanalysts love to think. We are deep thinkers but we also use our psychic capacity to contain affects and non-represented ideas to help others deal with conflicts and distress. Whilst trying to provide a better life for people, we offer a new opportunity to think differently, to behave in new patterns, and to manage affections in a more comprehensive way. This is our responsibility.

For as much as denial, depression, mania, and projection are some of the defence mechanisms present in life nowadays, we have specific tools to manage them. The analytic work has already been deeply tested and applied, leaving us with a strong awareness that we have something to heal psychic pain.

It is clear to me that the change to online setting will pose many questions to us psychoanalysts. As an international association, we will need to understand what has happened during these Covid-19 times in terms of setting, management of transference, the absence of the body, so on and so forth. If possible, we will build up research projects to enlighten our understanding of this period of change and adaptation.

On the other hand, the return to the offices and to face-to-face encounters will bring new challenges to us psychoanalysts. Some have already been discussed at our forums. How many will insist to stay with online sessions? How should a psychoanalyst deal with demands for a more flexible setting? How will be the first face-to-face encounters?

In my view, we might favour face-to-face sessions, as it brings much more to the humane encounter. After all, as stated by Isaacs Russell (2020): "True presence, as unpredictable, spontaneous and messy as it is, is irreplaceable" (p. 373). This will be, in my point of view, the North that will guide our next steps into the future. Let's see what will happen …

References

Birman, J. (1998). *Mal-estar na atualidade: a psicanálise e as novas formas de subjetivação* [*Current Malaise: Psychoanalysis and New Forms of Subjectivation*]. Rio de Janeiro: Civilização Brasileira.

Freud, S. (1916–17). *Introductory Lectures on Psycho-Analysis. S. E., 15–16.* London: Hogarth.

Isaacs Russell, G. (2020). Remote working during the pandemic: a Q&A with Gillian Isaacs Russell. *British Journal of Psychotherapy, 36*(3): 364–374. https://doi.org/10.1111/bjp.12581

Ogden, T. H. (2005). *This Art of Psychoanalysis: Dreaming Undreamt Dreams and Interrupted Cries.* London: Routledge.

Winnicott, D. W. (1962). The aims of psycho-analytical treatment. In: *The Maturational Processes and the Facilitating Environment* (pp. 166–170). New York: International Universities Press, 1965.

CHAPTER 7

From the glass slipper to the glass ceiling

Virginia Ungar

Introduction by João Seabra Diniz

Born in Buenos Aires, Argentina, Virginia Ungar was elected president of the International Psychoanalytical Association (IPA) in 2015 and took office in 2017. She is the first woman to hold this position.

Virginia presented this lecture in Lisbon in 2019 to a university audience, which made such an impact she was asked for interviews by the national press and television broadcasters.

From the outset she informs us that, in this chapter, she intends to relate her experiences in her new position with the historical moment we are experiencing. In the field of psychology, she understands that there have been many significant changes.

She considers of special importance the theme of misogyny, and the consideration of the inequality of opportunities that penalise women in relation to men. When she was elected president of the IPA, she was surprised by the impact this decision had, that for the first time this position was held by a woman. Despite all the changes that have taken place, she believes that women themselves are often dissuaded from considering the possibility of occupying certain posts when planning their careers. Obviously, there is an inner condition-ing that has not yet disappeared.

She presents the case of a patient under her analysis, which in her view illustrates several aspects of this complex problem. The traditional stories of Sleeping Beauty and Cinderella are used in this context to help understand the dynamics of the case and the title she gave to her work. She concludes with the statement that, at the pres-ent time, it is not enough to consider only the patient, or the interac-tion between patient and analyst, but it is also necessary to take into account the social context.

* * *

In this chapter, I would like to try to connect the experiences that I gar-ner in the position that I occupy, with the moment in history that we are living through in order to see if the latter can throw some light onto what is happening in our consulting rooms. I'll start by remembering an old idea of Ignacio Lewkowicz, an Argentine historian and philosopher, who died young in 2004. According to Lewkowicz, a political generation is not defined by a question of age but, rather, by thinking of a common question, over and beyond the different readings that we might have of that question. I dare to say in this context that our generation, or at least that part of it in the realm of psychoanalysis, has been buffeted (and therefore in a way defined) by intense changes in numerous areas in recent years. This, it goes without saying, especially embraces the ques-tion of gender.

In November 2018 I was invited as the guest speaker to the COWAP conference in Los Angeles where the subject was "Misogyny and the dialectic between the internal and external glass ceiling". I must confess that this invitation was a challenge for me and it made me read and study a lot on the subject, from gender theories to femi-nist economics. I would like to share with you some of the ideas that I presented in Los Angeles.

A number of factors have come together to make the theme of misogyny particularly relevant for me, besides the fact that the inequal-ity of opportunities that affect women with respect to men has been made visible in society over the past years. First, in 2015 I was elected to be president of the IPA, and in 2017 I took office, being the first woman to occupy this position since the foundation of the Association in 1910. Second, I was born and studied in Buenos Aires, Argentina, the city where I also live and work today. There, the women's movement is currently one of the most important political actors. *Ni Una Menos* (or "Not One (Woman) Less") as the movement is called, was born on 3 June, 2015 as a heart-rending collective cry in the face of gender violence in its most repugnant form: femicide. This movement has continued to grow and has expanded beyond the geographic limits of Argentina, involving itself in other regional issues and creating new expressions of feminism in the present day.

And then, in 2018, the debate on the legalisation of abortion in my country took an unexpected turn. On 13 June, the Chamber of Deputies debated the approval of a Law on the Decriminalisation of Abortion, preceded by two months of discussions in the commissions of the National Congress, with experts speaking in favour, and against, the proposal. The debate that particular day lasted for twenty-three hours and from very early on in the day until the morning of the following day, all through a very cold night. A million women gathered in the area of the Congress building waiting for the result.

Nevertheless, the events of the night of 13 June were witness to the birth of a new force in politics. The result, if only by a slim majority, was affirmative. The bill then passed to the second house, the Senate where, after a similarly cold night where two million people kept vigil in the rain, it was rejected, also by a small margin. In any case, there is no going back in the wake of this powerful mobilisation and the bringing into the limelight of an enormous public health problem.

When I was elected as president of the IPA, I was surprised by the impact that the decision to elect a woman to head the Association for the first time had.

In interviews in newspapers and on TV, I was asked why I thought the IPA had not, until then, had a female president. Although it was no easy task to formulate a generalised response, it was similarly impossible to ignore the dominant logic in modern societies and family configurations in which men were the centre and focus of public life. Following on this logic, the division of work between the sexes in the family dictated that political, institutional, and public activity was the (almost exclusive) ambit of men as was, to an even greater extent, any management that had to be done in these areas. In this way, for the hegemonic codes of the Victorian era, it was impossible for a woman to head institutions in general, and the IPA in particular.

Our times are not those of the beginning of the last century. And neither is the position of the women who work in our field today representative of that of the majority of women. Both of these are unquestionable. Being aware of these facts means that we do not deny the vulnerable position that women were in, and indeed are still in, in our society. Suffice to mention, receiving less pay for the same work at the same level of an organisation, enjoying fewer possibilities of accessing strategic and management positions, or the appearance of a "macho mentality" in our consulting rooms, even from women themselves. The latter never fails to surprise me and I see it often, including in young patients. I will take up this point again later when I present a clinical material.

Here, I believe it is worthwhile developing briefly, especially given that it is not a psychoanalytic term, the concept of the "glass ceiling", one that was coined within social sciences and, specifically, feminist economics. The glass ceiling is an invisible limitation which forms a barrier to women accessing the same positions as men in business, or indeed in society in general. It is determined by social relations and subjective preconceptions rooted in the collective subconscious. This, when coupled with concrete legislation (such as a lack of paternity law, at least in my country, Argentina) and ontologically verifiable evidence (the fact that there are fewer women in managerial positions) results in a vicious cycle which ends up justifying itself. Women do not gain access to certain spaces in society because "it is not in our nature".

To the glass ceiling, we could add the concept of the "glass wall" where, instead of talking about the impossibility of upward mobility to access the same as men do, we talk about those invisible mechanisms which impede horizontal movement for female workers into occupations which have traditionally been associated with men: becoming a construction worker, football commentator, or governor, for example.

Both coordinates contribute to the organisation of reality, but they also put a check on us internally, where the pressures are twofold and effective: when one sees that most of the people who manage companies are men, it is highly probable that a woman would not imagine that she could access this area. And for this reason she does not plan a career in this area. Furthermore, as women decide and choose to undertake careers in the greater care sector (teacher, nurse …), this implies that the idea takes hold that women are only of use in certain sectors.

When I present the clinical material, I would like to address the question of those places which women occupy for society and, moreover, the possible unconscious fantasies which are involved in that situation. The glass ceiling is, needless to say, a crystallisation of a social asymmetry, its justification is based on fallacies, but it has both concrete and social consequences as it becomes ingrained in the individuality of each person as part of the unconscious belief system. And it is precisely here that we enter into what I would like to speak about today: the internal glass ceiling.

Before I present the clinical experience, I would like to share with you what I understand to be the external and the internal, focusing on the latter. A ceiling, as something above our heads, tends to limit upward movement. If we think of the external as the area of the social in the greater sense, the glass ceiling is, frankly speaking, the expression of patriarchal society. That is to say, a coercion which understands as natural the fact that women occupy a space in the world which is not only different, but also inferior to that of men.

This glass ceiling functions with such subtle mechanisms that it is constantly being absorbed by our subjectivities, creating a second space of limitation, this time internally: our internal glass ceiling is the stopping up of desire, the thought that there are certain objectives that we cannot even desire to have or attain, or the realignment of our own desire in order to adapt to a hegemonic model of women in a state of submission.

To look further into the concept, I am now going to present a detailed material from a session of the analysis with a married woman who has four children. In it, I would like to give examples of the unconscious collaboration of a woman within a patriarchal alliance. Often, and even in the case of successful and apparently independent women, there is a consent to an unconscious alliance with protective characteristics where the price paid is the surrendering of the possibility of forging one's own path. That common fantasy amongst female patients of obtaining protection sometimes evolves into their own limitation of developing themselves as individuals.

What follows is a vignette from a session with Ms A, a clued-up, slim, elegant, sophisticated dresser who is forty-seven years old. She started analysis three years before this session. She has a university degree but does not work in the field. She dedicates herself to the care of her four children (two daughters and two sons) and the family home. Her husband is the CEO of a multinational corporation and is very successful in his work.

> When she arrived for her Monday session she was smiling, as usual, but she looked pale and tense. She kept a tight hold on her purse. She lay down on the couch and started talking about how bad she felt because her husband was travelling for work and her nine-year-old daughter, the youngest of her four kids, said to her at breakfast that she misses her dad when he leaves.
>
> She immediately spoke of a "horrible" dream she had the night before, in which someone was coming in, but she didn´t have any images … She glimpsed something like a shadow by her bed, a figure, but she couldn't make out its shape … She felt something like a breeze on her body, something soft, like the air being displaced by someone moving nearby. She suddenly woke up, fearful.
>
> The patient associated with a time when she spent some summer holidays with her grandmother at the family beach house near the sea. She was a little girl and her granny told her about her husband who had left her when Ms A's mother was a little girl.
>
> At that point of the session I had an association with Hamlet, of the appearance of the ghost of the father, and after waiting for a while I interpreted that her anxiety caused by her husband's trip abroad apparently took her back to her childhood.
>
> She said that she never understood why her grandmother used to speak about her grandfather as if he were a saint, a great man … and he had abandoned his wife and children … She added that this is a constant pattern in her family, her father was always away from home because he was a commercial pilot.
>
> When I asked her about possible associations with the dream, she started to say that during the weekend they watched The Godfather Part I on TV, and that she loved it, there's a scene that was very moving: when he, Marlon Brando, asked Diane Keaton to marry him. She said: "It's so romantic! … I told my husband that he never did that

to me, and he said that I always complain." [I remembered Marlon Brando and Diane Keaton, but not the scene the patient mentioned.] "I find that movie fascinating, the actors, Marlon Brando, James Caan, and the other one ... everything. I'm thinking of something, but I'm embarrassed to tell you. [Silence] Well, when it ended, I thought, 'I would have loved to be part of a family like that one, the women were always well protected.' I know that it's the Mafia, but he's so strong, he takes care of everybody ..."

I then interpreted that, if she was embarrassed to talk about this thought she had, we could go back to the dream and that the breeze that seemed to be left by someone who was leaving, who was threatening, brings back a fear that seems to be very old and hard to put into words. It's a breeze, a shadow, and then what emerges is a yearning for protection at any personal cost, like the one the Mafia brings.

The patient answered almost immediately that she couldn't believe that she could want to be part of the Mafia, that this is what she felt.

The session continued, but we'll leave it there. I believe that the material lets us see how the patient helps to prop up, in her internal world, an agreement with the tenets of a patriarchal society which many years ago assigned the role of strength, protection, and supply to the men and to the women that of weakness, of being in danger and at the mercy of "bad men".

This patient had decided to abandon her professional development to dedicate herself to her children and her husband, whose work led him to travel continuously, leaving her to look after their four children as well as to organise his social agenda.

This session also laid bare the issue of transgenerational transmission: men abandon the family and "make their own lives" only to return later and be accepted, in many cases leaving women unprotected.

Going further, to a level accessed by sustained analytic work, Ms A ends up expressing, together with her fear of being left alone, a desire to belong to a Mafia family which could protect her, appearing to be surprised by the fact that she expresses this fantasy verbally. She seems to have an idea that she could have had a life which was different from the one she is living and I believe this is why she feels ashamed when she expresses openly her desire to be part of a Mafia family.

Similarly, in the transferential relationship it is not clear to which world *I* belong and how I am going to take what she has to say. She would seem to "know" that for women there could be at least two ways of inhabiting the world today: that of the independent women struggling for equality and that of "traditional" women who have to be maintained by men and do housework which is neither recognised nor remunerated.

Here we can see in action an unconscious "mafia" alliance with the "protective" aspects of the man, her husband, something that contains—as in the matryoshka (or Russian) doll, a man's family history and which offers her protection at a price: that she should relinquish any personal desire for development. I say "protective" in quotation marks because it is not the good Kleinian object; it is, conversely, destructive and malevolent in its aim to subjugate.

In that way, the glass ceiling can remind us of another object which has an enduring cultural heritage: Cinderella's glass slipper. In the folk tale, the prince tries to find the owner of the glass slipper that he found on the steps outside the ball, testing it on the feet of all the women of the kingdom until he finds the small foot that fits into it. As we all know, the owner of the slipper corresponds to a certain model of woman: the small foot of a blonde, white, slim, and delicate one, thus excluding all those women who do not fit that supposed incarnation of the ideal which holds strong to the present day, even if the first versions of the tale can be traced back hundreds of years.

The patient's fantasy (expressed in the associations she makes from the dream) is that of forming a Mafia alliance and refers to an unconscious pact with the subjugating elements of the father–godfather–prince–husband figure which brings about the submission of the woman in return for protection at any cost, including the suppressing of one's own desires.

In this sense, the play between the figure of the Father and that of the Godfather, Don Corleone, is interesting—the latter protects and gives shelter in exchange for an eternal payment—as is the patient's lapsus (which I only later became aware of on reconstructing the session) with respect to Marlon Brando that results in her leaving aside another man (Al Pacino in the film). Similarly, my association with the ghost of Hamlet's father opens up a path towards even more possible meanings.

We may also consider the possibility of it being related to a childish fantasy and, as such, we could continue interconnecting the case with the archetypes which fairy tales produce. In *Sleeping Beauty*, the princess sleeps for a hundred years until a prince arrives, gives her a kiss, and takes her off to his kingdom. He fulfils the active role whilst she is simply beautiful, giving her consent to marriage—and, therefore, entering into adult life—without passing through the process of adolescence, without revolution, or desire. Coming back to *Cinderella*, we also come face to face with certain stereotypes concerning the feminine which are socially loaded with the protagonist being forced to work in the house, only talking to animals. As she is beautiful and obliging, the Fairy Godmother comes and lets her go to the ball until midnight, a ball where the prince will choose between the thousands of girls who want him—as he is a prince, that is to say, rich—to make one his wife. After a short dance with Cinderella and without even speaking with her, he falls in love but, when the clock strikes twelve, she runs from the ball so as not to be identified as a poor girl who normally dresses in rags and all the prince is left with is a glass slipper. Only a beautiful girl with a diminutive foot could be the owner of this slipper. He does not know her name, nor does he remember her entirely; he is only interested in the slipper fitting her.

It was the slipper that particularly caught my attention, not only because it harks back to a classical fetish, but also because it is connected to the concept of the place that each and every one of us occupies in the world. This slipper, made of glass just like the ceiling, defines us in the patriarchal vision of a defenceless woman who must be chosen and saved by a man. The ceiling, which is also the head, is internalised and blocks off our desires and aspirations: it makes us want to be slim and delicate, and ends up imposing on us a certain vision of ourselves in which we are only of worth if chosen by a man to whom we then owe loyalty in exchange for protection, often paying the price of the surrendering of personal development.

To conclude, I would like now to share with you some final reflections: we are living in a very different era from the one in which psychoanalysis was born. For us, as analysts today, it is no longer possible to focus only on the patient, or in the interaction between patient and analyst. Today we also have to take into account the social context.

In this respect, my intention in presenting this chapter was to reflect upon the interaction between the factors that determine the internal and external glass ceiling, focusing on the internal factors, which relate to the everyday work with my patients.

Part II

Theory of psychoanalytic technique

CHAPTER 8

Towards a two-track model for psychoanalysis

Howard B. Levine

Introduction by Rui Aragão Oliveira

Howard Levine's first visit to Lisbon was part of a colloquium on "Psychoanalysis in the global era" in 2013, as part of an effort to revive a community of professionals and students who, like the entire population, were devastated by the serious political and economic crisis that dominated the country, and which required a difficult financial intervention by the Troika, with tremendous social consequences and widespread impoverishment.

His communication is still remembered today for its intensity and vivacity, his ability to energise different generations, including a thorough study of historical thinking of some of the main authors of psychoanalysis. His communication skills, accessibility, and friendliness have sparked a contagious enthusiasm, which has, in turn, made him a regular and inspiring presence.

This chapter of enormous richness deals with the transformation in psychoanalytic thinking—the transformation of the object of psychoanalytic study, the transformation of the implications in clinical interpretation and of the factors of analytical cure, as well as the transformation of the demands placed on the psychoanalyst and inevitably on his or her own training as a psychoanalyst.

With a profound knowledge of the work of Wilfred Bion and André Green, Howard Levine presents us with a transformational trajectory where the psychic work of the analyst is based on a tertiary conceptual axis that includes floating attention (from an intrapsychic perspective, on content analysis), and countertransference (from an intersubjective perspective, with the analysis of the relationship and of the container), subordinating them to a broader and more complex range of operations, in which psychoanalytic imagination and creativity are prominent.

This text, having been published in the Portuguese journal *Revista Portuguesa de Psicanálise*, has become a classic that frequently features in the training programmes of Portuguese psychoanalysts.

* * *

In my paper, "Creating analysts, creating analytic patients" (Levine, 2010), I wrote about the need for a "two track model" of psychoanalysis. Although the terminology may have been new, this was not an "original" concept. It derives in large part from my reading of André Green, particularly his paper given at the London International Journal of Psychoanalysis Congress (Green, 1975) in which he drew a clear distinction between neuroses on the one hand and borderline or "limit cases" (*etats limites*) on the other. Perhaps the most important thing that I took away from Green's paper was the realisation that each of these categories is based upon a different and distinct underlying psychic organisation and may imply and require a different understanding and approach to analytic listening and technique.

Green's paper has become a classic and is foundational, as one of many writings that have called specific attention to this discontinuity (caesura)—I might even say, fracture—in analytic theory. It challenges us to widen the net of our thinking, to build a conceptual bridge that is truly psychoanalytic across this divide, and to work out the clinical and theoretical implications of the duality that Green brings to our attention. In so doing, however, Green was of course "merely"—and I use that designation ironically, because of the powerful and far-reaching effects of his work on our thinking—following upon the work of Freud, who eventually came to recognise that while his first topography provided us with the clinical and theoretical tools needed to understand and treat neurotic patients, his formulations were not sufficient to understand and address certain kinds of unconscious guilt and negative therapeutic reactions, pathological narcissism, and the consequences of pre-verbal and massive psychic trauma. In short, all those patients and difficulties that lay "beyond the pleasure principle" (Freud, 1920g). Put another way, the first topography addressed that which was organised, formed, but hidden in the psyche, while the second topography, the "structural theory", allowed us to better understand and address the very process of psychic formation, the movement from unrepresented to represented mental states.

Time does not permit me to elaborate upon this, but I will briefly note that Freud's shift towards structural theory (his second topography) moved analytic thinking away from a mode of theory that was heavily based on veridical, sensory-empirical data and representations (Scarfone, 2011)—for example, the unconscious as formed, verbalisable but disguised or repressed contents—to one that was based on metapsychological principles—for example, the id as force in search of content and containment; construction, myth and the playful, creative and self-generating work of *Nachträglichkeit* (*après coup*).

This perspective and its implications for technique were absent in my own training, which took place under the dominance of North American ego psychology, where Freud's (1923b) introduction of the structural theory was seen as more or less continuous with, and a natural extension of, the topographic theory that had gone before it. There was little attention given to unrepresented states or recognition of the ways or the extent to which the second topography shattered what had been a homogeneous and unitary vision of psychoanalysis (Green, 2005). But, in fact, the effect of Freud's reformulation was much like that of placing a glass crystal in the path of a clear beam of light. It diffracted analytic theory into multiple components: ego psychology, Klein, Winnicott, Lacan, Bion, etc. Contemporary psychoanalytic theory and practice, with its comparative thrust and more eclectic bent—the very subject that brings us together today—is still trying to understand and work through the tensions and consequences that followed upon this change.

Rather than emphasising and appreciating the discontinuities between neurosis and what lay beyond, the analysis that I grew up with attempted to maintain the vision of a unified theory in which almost, if not all relevant psychic occurrences could be attributed to the interplay of structurally organised unconscious motivation, anxiety, phantasy, and defence. These assumptions placed analysts in a paradoxical, cognitively dissonant, and often impossible position vis-à-vis the actual patients they were seeing. I have already described (Levine, 2010) how suppositions about analysability did not successfully predict outcome or conform to the actuality of which patients were analysable by which analysts. In regard to the treatment of adults who had been sexually abused as children, I have also recounted (Levine, 1990) how theory led me to (mistakenly) expect that analysis of defences and reliance on the patient's developing capacity for free association would eventually and predictably lead to the emergence of associations within the patient's discourse that pointed, albeit in disguised or cryptic fashion, to the salient pathogenic traumatic events.

In retrospect, although some of the difficulty undoubtedly came from my misunderstanding or misapplication of ego psychological principles, the reason that things were not working out as my then theory predicted was that it was encumbered by a number of unrecognised and unstated assumptions. One such assumption was that the relevant and sought after analytic material was potentially verbalisable, but repressed or otherwise defended against. That is, although this material was unconscious, it was assumed to be psychically represented, elaborated and embedded in narrative structures, and connected to other psychic elements by associative chains. If this was the case, then with free association by the patient and sufficient analysis of resistance—that is, with patience on the part of the analyst and attention to the anxieties inherent in the analytic situation and relationship and/or the defences those anxieties evoked in regard to the emergence of certain feelings, fantasies, and wishes–these hidden and disguised thoughts, feelings, and fantasies would make themselves known by virtue of their pressure on the patient's more accessible thoughts, feelings and fantasies. Interpretation and analysis of defence would then initiate a process of working-through and conflict resolution that would strengthen the therapeutic alliance and help the patient to tolerate the underlying anxieties and eventually come to use the potential of the analytic setting for the reworking of conflicts and psychic growth.

As you no doubt recognise, this is a traditional description of the analytic process, which I categorised under the heading of the archaeological model (Levine, 2010). It is admirably suited to the treatment of neurotic patients and is predominantly derived from Freud's first topography, according to which analytic praxis was based on the pleasure–unpleasure principle, dream interpretation, the treatment of hysterical neurosis, and the psychopathology of everyday life. It is also consistent with how Freud was usually portrayed as working analytically. That is, he would make a dramatic interpretation of some forgotten childhood (often sexual) event with the assurance and conviction that his reconstruction was historically correct.[1] The implications of his 1937 paper, in which he allowed that reconstructions could often be psychically and therapeutically valuable even if not historically correct, and acknowledged that an historically incorrect construction could stand in for and assume the dynamic function of a recovered accurate memory, had not yet been fully appreciated or integrated into analytic thinking (Freud, 1937d).[2]

As I wrote in 2010:

> the archaeological model was best suited for situations in which psychic elements have achieved representation and have been more or less symbolically invested and associatively linked to one another. It is this symbolic tie to dangerous and/or unacceptable wishes, feelings, fantasies and needs that leads to the familiar situation of psychic elements becoming enmeshed in conflict, undergoing the vicissitudes of repression or other defensive disguise and remaining hidden from conscious awareness, while continuing to exert a pressure on the psyche until the conflicts they are involved in are discovered and worked through to some resolution. (p. 1387)

---

[1] In the case of the Wolf Man, for example, he concluded that the wolf dream and its associations implied the occurrence of an actual event (Freud, 1918b).

[2] I have discussed these implications elsewhere (Levine, 2011).

The archaeological model worked well enough for the treatment of many neurotics, but proved increasingly problematic when applied to what was then called the "widening scope" of analytic patients; what most of us would today call our everyday caseloads! It remains an open question of the extent to which the nature of patients seeking analytic treatment has changed, or our understanding of the depth and complexity of their pathology has deepened, since the time of Freud's first theory. Whatever the case, I can attest to the fact that in almost forty years of practice and supervision, the so-called "good neurotic" patient has proven to be the exception rather than the rule.

In the many instances where non-neurotic and even manifestly psychotic cases were successfully treated within—we might say despite—this archaeological formulation of the curative process, success was less often due solely to the rigorous application of an archaeological theory of technique and more often due to the additional influence of "non-technical factors", such as the analyst's unique subjectivity or intuitive response to the patient's needs, the inspired application of what used to be referred to as the "art of psychoanalysis", engaging the patient in a search for meaning almost independent of the nature of the discovered meaning itself or the salutary effect of non-specific therapeutic factors in the analytic relationship—for example, consistency, empathy, non-judgemental concern, maintenance of an analytic frame and attitude, etc.

But success in these non-neurotic cases was often difficult to come by and as you can imagine—and as many of you have experienced first hand—having a theory that does not conform to clinical reality or help you to adequately understand or function in the clinical situations in which you find yourself can prove very frustrating. And, as impasses, treatment difficulties, and failures accumulate, in either one's practice, or even worse, in one's own personal analysis, such a theory can only be discouraging. I believe it is this discouragement and the absence of an analytic theory that included the effective understanding and treatment of many patients who presented for treatment that has added to the sociocultural difficulties in case finding and building an analytic practice.

This seemed to be the case in the US. After an initial period of excessive optimism, expectation, and over-application, archaeological analysis:

- proved increasingly restricted in its application (e.g., analytic treatment of psychotic or psychosomatic cases has all but disappeared in North America)
- was challenged by alternative analytic formulations (self psychology, infant development based theories, the relational school, etc.)
- ceded the therapeutic field to non-analytic forms of treatment (CBT, DBT, etc.).

In some quarters, analysis began to lose its specificity and was seen as a kind of "super psychotherapy" aimed more at conflict resolution and better adaptation than at growth of the psyche. (It is not that these are unimportant or not part of the outcome of a successful analytic treatment. It is that when the central goal of the analysis is excessively taken over by pragmatic therapeutic concerns, there is apt to be a loss of the power and dare I say magic that is inherent and unique to a true analytic engagement.) Residues of this latter shift can still be detected in those candidates who apply for psychoanalytic training with the aim, not of going on to become practising analysts, but of becoming better psychotherapists. This may be a problem that is more immediate in the US, but is apt to occur in any region where selection standards come under pressure as recruitment of candidates fail to meet institutional expectations and needs.

This then was the background of my 2010 article, which wound up reflecting the confluence of two somewhat different streams of intention. The first was didactic and pragmatic. As case finding became increasingly difficult for both candidates and graduate analysts, I had turned my attention to trying to identify and understand why this might be so and to see if I could develop some concrete suggestions concerning the timing and working-through of the suggestion to intensify the frequency of treatment. As part of this investigation, I conducted a number of clinical seminars for candidates and recent graduates on intensifying the treatment, converting patients from therapy to analysis and developing analytic patients. Some of the more pragmatic, clinical considerations, recommendations, and conclusions of that work are included in the 2010 article.

But while this direction was one I thought useful, I began to realise that a broader and more profound reorganisation of my thinking was required and indeed seemed to be quietly taking place. Increasingly, I began to feel that a significant part of the problem of case finding involved analysts' inability to feel that they could apply analysis to the kind of patients, problems, and settings with which they were confronted. Even more so, as treatment of psychosis, psychosomatic, borderline, and other primitive personality disorders was ceded to non-analytic modalities, it seemed harder and harder for analysts to think analytically about these patients and their problems. Consequently, I came to believe that in order for an analyst to venture into these relatively uncharted waters, it was necessary to have in mind a guiding theory that covered the necessary territory and that an analyst could feel was truly psychoanalytic. This led to my articulation of the second track, which dealt more with catalysing and participating in the creation of mind and meaning than with uncovering what was pre-existing but hidden. It was for this reason that I designated this second track as transformational.

The transformational model "centers upon the functioning of the mind of the analyst as a part of the analytic dyad in the creation and/or strengthening of psychic elements rather than, or in addition to, their uncovering or discovery" (Levine, 2010, p. 1388). It:

> emphasizes that psychoanalysis is a pair specific, two-person activity that is liable to be as much if not more about the creation of symbols, thoughts, feelings and the unconscious than it is about their uncovering or discovery. In some situations, the task of the analyst may be less about analysing defenses or uncovering hidden or disguised meanings and more about lending one's psyche to the work of facilitating the patient's development of thoughts, feelings and mental states; of naming and elaborating these newly formed psychic elements and linking them to other components, in the mind of either participant or in the intersubjective mental space that lies between them. In short, of "binding the inchoate, and in containing it within a form" (Green, 1975, p. 10) and working "with the patient in a double operation: to give a container to his content and a content to his container" (Green, 1975, p. 8). (Levine, 2010, p. 1388)

The transformational model opens up the possibility that despite little or no evidence of a therapeutic alliance or a split between the patient's observing and experiencing ego, an analytic process may still be present and ongoing. However, that process may have to be sustained within the mind of the analyst, rather than within the patient, or in the discourse between the two, sometimes for considerably lengthy periods of time. While this places a greater burden and responsibility upon the analyst and the countertransference and may increase the risk of dependency, suggestion, and compliance, it also widens the scope of application of analysis and offers the analyst the possibility, and even comfort, of a theory that can bridge the divide between the borderline and the neurotic–normal.[3]

Such a theory holds out the promise of extending classical thinking and allowing:

> analysts to think and act analytically in the face of unrepresented as well as represented mental states, disorganized as well as organized sectors of their patients' psyches, and autistic, psychotic and borderline phenomena as well as neurotic-normal phenomena. The addition of the transformational track completes a more comprehensive theory that can be applied to a wider scope of patients and will therefore help in the matter of case finding, as it emboldens analysts to encourage even "sicker" patients to enter into analysis and more intensive treatments.
>
> With the expectation that each analysis or analytic therapy will require an unconscious, joint improvisation, the process will begin from the initial contact, with the analyst—and hopefully, but not necessarily, the patient—wondering and discovering what and how this pair will begin to improvise together, unconsciously, spontaneously. In initiating treatment, the "diagnostic questions" then shift from the traditional focus on the individual patient and his or her ego capacities to the functioning of the mind of the analyst in response to the patient and to the analytic pair. (Levine, 2010, p. 1389)

The transformational theory that I am describing derives from, and is consistent with, the work of Bion, Ferro, Green, the Paris Psychosomatic

---

[3] And as Donnet (2009) has noted, in extreme cases, the inadvertent provision of an "analytic false self" may be the best that one can help the patient to achieve.

School, César and Sara Botella, René Roussillon, etc. It hypothesises the existence of unrepresented, proto-mental states and a level of registration that could be called "pre-psychic".

It is interesting to note that the distinction between pre-psychic and psychic, between unrepresented registrations and represented mental states, is analogous to one that Freud (1900a) hypothesised in chapter seven of *The Interpretation of Dreams*, when he attempted to distinguish between a system for registering perceptions (Pcpt.) and a system for creating and registering memories (Mnem.):[4]

> We shall suppose that a system in the front of the [psychic] apparatus receives the perceptual stimuli but retains no trace of them and thus has no memory, while behind it there lies a second system which transforms the momentary excitations of the first system into permanent traces. (p. 538)

In Freud's view, the system Pcpt., which is without memory, "provides our consciousness with the whole multiplicity of sensory qualities" (p. 539), while memories, especially the memories of earliest childhood which have made the greatest impressions upon us are themselves, for the most part, unconscious. This dual registration theory and its evolution in Freud's work and in psychoanalytic theory has important implications for our consideration of the two track model, as it underlies the idea of two categories of unconscious phenomena, the unformed or unrepresented unconscious, which consists of a non-evolving and not yet evolved field of sensori-somatic inscriptions or traces, and the dynamic unconscious, which consists of formed but repressed mental elements.[5]

The transformational theory also reflects the evolution of the theory of countertransference in which the term first appeared in Freud as a potential interference; then broadened to encompass all of the analyst's reactions to the patient and the analytic situation-countertransference in its "totalistic" sense; began to be recognised as a necessary and valuable

---

[4] I am indebted to Sara Botella (2010) for pointing this out, and to André Green (2012) for calling this to our attention.

[5] See Levine et al. (2013) for an extensive discussion of these issues.

receptive attitude in the analyst; and found its most radical position in the assertion of Paula Heimann (1950) that the countertransference of the analyst actually reflects and belongs to the personality of the patient. When combined with Bion's (1962, 1970) assertion of the potentially communicative dimension of projective identification, and his theory of alpha function and container/contained, as well as an appreciation of the protective, homeostatic dimension of representation and elaboration of narrative, the concept of countertransference taken in its widest possible sense finally emerges as a component of the analyst's subjectivity on the way to becoming absorbed into a truly intersubjective field theory and formulation of psychic development and the analytic process.

As Green (2012) so aptly put it, when confronted with non-neurotic patients or areas of the mind: "The countertransference makes up for what has not been (or could not be) lived: it is about inventing the possible" (p. 1243).

This trajectory can also be viewed from the perspective of psychic reality: what began for Freud as empirically observable and historically verifiable "facts"—traumatic childhood experiences that were repressed and otherwise disguised, because of the anxiety that they were associated with—and then expanded to include repressed or disguised childhood phantasies, wishes and fears—that is, "facts" of psychic reality—have increasingly become seen as "markers" of pre- and proto-psychic sensori-motor inscriptions and disturbances, inchoate and barely organised somatic turbulences, that are in search of subjectivisation, temporalisation, verbalisation, and containment, in the form of one of many possible narrative "dialects" (Ferro, 2002). In clinical terms, positivism yields to phenomenology; observation and deduction are assisted by intuition and inspiration; empiricism is supplemented and even supplanted by creativity, invention, and imagination.

It is my belief that the addition of the transformational model to the archaeological model will offer analysts:

> a more comprehensive theory that can be applied to a wider scope of patients. It should therefore help in the matter of case finding, as it emboldens analysts to encourage even "sicker" patients to enter into analysis and more intensive treatments. (Levine, 2010, p. 1389)

Furthermore, it:

- Supports the view that assessment of prognosis and analysability is pair specific for any given dyad.
- Requires the consideration of analyst-centred variables along with patient-centred variables in the determination of the treatment setting and the assessment of analysability.
- Emphasises the emergence of spontaneous, unconscious, interactive, and intersubjective processes of transformation that allow for the creation and strengthening of psychic representations, symbols, and meaningful chains of associations.
- And underscores the fact that "the creation of a given analytic patient will be a function of the degree to which the analyst will be able to internally create and maintain him or herself as an analyst with and for that particular patient" (Levine, 2010, p. 1390). This makes central the inter-affectivity and potential interactions and emotional connections that may develop between any given analyst–patient pair and implicates the mind of the analyst as the crucial location of the analytic process, especially in the treatment of psychotic, psycho-somatic, primitive narcissistic, and borderline patients.

In the 2010 paper, I offered a number of technical recommendations that are useful to keep in mind when considering a shift from therapy to analysis or recommending that the treatment be intensified. These included:

- Maintaining an analytic perspective and keeping alive an internal sense of an analytic process from the very beginning and throughout contact with the patient.
- Keeping open the possibility that any negative assessment of the patient, including wishes to send the patient elsewhere or for non-analytic forms of treatment may be transference–countertransference responses that need to be understood—perhaps initially internally and silently by the analyst—from an analytic perspective.
- De-centring oneself from the status quo of an ongoing therapy in order to take a "second look" at the treatment process, re-assess

potential areas of stasis and reconsider whether the treatment structure and setting is optimal for the patient's needs.

- Being sensitive to possible changes in mood, accessibility, aliveness, or level of discourse, etc., that may ebb and flow with gaps between sessions. Commenting on and exploring such shifts may allow the patient to recognise the ways in which the gaps between sessions may be impeding the treatment process or unconsciously contributing to regression or stasis.

- Recognising the importance of offering the patient a first-hand experience of the value of analytic exploration and interpretation before recommending an intensification in the meeting schedule, so that the matter of session frequency can be reflected on in the light of personal experience rather than resting predominantly on the authority of the analyst.

I do not have additional clinical principles to offer you at this time. These, if they exist, will have to emerge in the course of future discussions and case studies. However, I do not wish to end without speaking, albeit briefly, about some clinical material and so I will offer two brief sketches that may help indicate how the broad concepts and principles I have presented today may be applied.

The first case is that of a middle-aged man with severe "social anxiety", obsessions and phobias that was brought to me for consultation by an analyst–colleague. Mr A, as I shall call him, was in a twice weekly, face-to-face psychotherapy because of his crippling symptoms. He had had a very traumatic childhood that included repeated homosexual seductions by an older boy that had become condensed in his mind with humiliating experiences in school, a close friend and a relative who each committed suicide and, in adolescence, a cousin who died in a car accident after an intense day of drinking and recreational drug use. What gradually emerged in the therapy was the extent to which Mr A's internal world was filled with violence and erotised sadistic fantasies that terrorised him, filled him with intense shame, and were directly connected to his phobias and social withdrawal.

When I was first consulted, the analyst had been responding to Mr A's panic attacks and crippling symptoms by referring him for medication and offering encouragement, structure, support, and real-ity testing. This represented a shift away from her more customary explorative/interpretive stance and it was meeting with only limited success. Our initial conversations helped the analyst to step back from her enmeshment in what appeared to be an unproductive transference–countertransference enactment and rethink what might be going on from within a more analytic frame. This "second look" allowed her first to re-engage herself more analytically in thinking about the material and then to more openly address the patient's shame and terror that if he revealed the content and extent of his erotic sadistic fantasies, he would be seen as "crazy," "disgusting" or "perverted".

As these fears were named and addressed, the treatment began to get untracked. The patient recalled his sexual seduction, expressed fears of being destructively or seductively out of control, and revealed how much he blamed himself for his friend's car accident. His affect became richer, his associations freer and more productive, and the sessions became more alive. For example, on the eve of a holiday break, Mr A talked of his fascination with the aborigines in an Australian film he had seen, described it as depicting "a dark and savage magical place" that was their "real world" and linked it to the artefacts he had bought to use as inspira-tion for a novel that he was trying to write. He then described how the physical presence of the artefacts in his study had become so terrifying that he had to put them out of sight in order to remain in the room.

The analyst silently understood this as communicating how inter-ested Mr A had become in the dark and primitive side of his psyche, a part of himself that the treatment was helping him to explore and try to understand, but also how terrifyingly overwhelming and real his fantasies could feel to him.

An unsaturated interpretation about Mr A's interest in, and fear of, the savage and primitive led to associations about his cousin's car crash, the gruesome way his uncle killed himself and left himself to be found, and Mr A's envy of what he assumed was the freedom and abandonment of his cousin's sexual relationship with the girlfriend, who also died in the car crash. The analyst responded by noting that the patient felt his cousin had found his soulmate, but then they died, to which Mr A mov-ingly confessed how guilty he felt for participating in the drinking and drug use that preceded the accident, how he could not tear himself away from his cousin's coffin at the funeral, and then in the session burst into tears. This ushered in a long delayed mourning reaction for the cousin and further analysis of the patient's sense of guilt.

Over the following weeks, the analyst helped the patient notice the changes in his affective availability and how it seemed to intensify with therapeutic contact and wane in the gaps between sessions. This led to the analyst's wondering if there would be some advantage to adding a third or even fourth session to try to maintain momentum and keep the affect alive. Although this tentative suggestion brought forward intense dreams of homosexual pleasure and of a building that looked lovely from the distance but proved to be only a façade covering rot and decay, dreams the analyst could then interpret as fearful responses to what a more intensified treatment schedule might reveal, the patient was ultimately able to accept the importance of more frequent sessions and the analysis deepened further.

The second patient, Mr B, was an even more dysfunctional and traumatised middle-aged man who had been homosexually seduced by a foster father and other figures as a child. Years before beginning treatment, Mr B had impulsively ended a troubled marriage and exiled himself from his three children. Then, he killed a woman in a car accident and his life broke down completely in an onslaught of primitive guilt, fear, and self-hatred. At the time I was consulted, Mr B was beginning the second year of a twice weekly, face-to-face psychotherapy with a young analytic candidate, who practised in a rural area and had limited access to referrals. The candidate was being pressured by his Training Committee to begin a first control and was somehow hoping that despite the patient's life circumstances—Mr B had been unemployed and non-functional for several years, was phobic about appearing in public and virtually housebound, unhappily remarried to an impulsive and sometimes abusive woman and spent all of his time caring for a severely regressed, autistic-sounding adolescent step-son—that this patient would become his first "official" training case.

Prior to beginning the consultation, the candidate had been unsuccessfully trying to make empathic contact with Mr B by emphasising the many traumas, losses, and betrayals in his history and encouraging him to re-engage with the world. In contrast, the first phase of the consultation helped the candidate to better understand and address the enormity of Mr B's unconscious guilt, self-blame, need for punishment, and fear of his own rage. This shift in therapeutic focus, away from the trauma induced by "bad objects" to the patient's internal, psychic sense of agency, guilt, and murderous, destructive wishes soon began to produce a palpable change in the sessions. Mr B then described the car accident in which the woman was killed in a new way. The candidate learned that it did not take place on a clear, sunny day, but that the weather conditions and visibility were poor. The patient was driving his young children somewhere, and two of them were quarrelling in the back seat. The third was fussing in the front seat and when he refused to get something for Mr B from the glove compartment, Mr B irritably reached for it himself. It was at that moment that the accident occurred and the woman was killed.

This new version of the event astounded the candidate and allowed him to better explore and analyse the patient's guilt and self blame, and sort out the difference between a terrible and tragic accident and an act of intentional murder. It also allowed him to re-examine Mr B's failure to defend himself at trial, his wish to be sent to prison, and his depressive withdrawal and collapse from the perspective of self-blame, need for self punishment, and wish to avoid anger and conflict at all costs. This led in turn to associations to, and examination of, Mr B's guilt and self-blame for the initial break-up of his childhood family (at eight years old); his feeling that he must submit to the sexual abuse of his foster father and brothers as punishment and confirmation of his worthlessness; etc.

After several months, the treatment had deepened considerably and the candidate decided to apply to have the case considered as an official training case. I should add that in his Society, which is independent and not part of the International Psychoanalytical Association (IPA) or the American Psychoanalytic Association (APsaA), candidates are required to have two training cases at a minimum of three to four times per week, but may request approval for a third case that is deemed "atypical". The response of the training committee was that he should begin to see if he could arrange to add a third session. It was at this point that I intervened.

While I am very much in favour of intensifying the frequency of treatments, I felt that there was nothing in the material to indicate that there was an internal, unconscious pressure to do so. The motivation seemed to be coming from requirements of the training committee and their view of the candidate's training needs. In this case, especially given that the patient's childhood was filled with disregard of his needs and interests and his being narcissistically and sexually appropriated for the use and needs of others, I felt that to use him once more for the needs of others—that is, the candidate—could be dangerously unproductive. Would it be, or be felt, as forcing him to submit once more and sacrifice what was in his best interests to the rapacious needs of others? Would a poorly timed intensification of meetings overload and outstrip his capacity to use the setting, a capacity that had just been newly mobilised in recent months?

I raised these questions and concerns with the candidate, who then reported them to the training committee. A meeting was held to discuss the case that included the candidate and myself. We eventually agreed that acceptance of the case as an "atypical" control should be considered on the merits of the treatment and not be contingent on the setting being forced to meet an external administrative requirement about frequency. This would allow the case to continue at its present frequency. The question of increasing the frequency, should it become indicated or useful, would better be dealt with in relation to the case itself and at a time that the process indicated would be useful to consider. What I wish to convey in offering this second example is that despite our conviction about, and enthusiasm for, psychoanalysis and the intensification of the treatment process, the latter must always be considered in the current context and tailored to fit the needs and capacities of the patient and the pair.

References

Bion, W. R. (1962). *Learning from Experience*. London: Heinemann.

Bion, W. R. (1970). *Attention and Interpretation*. London: Heinemann.

Botella, S. (2010). De la mémoire du ça [From the memory of that]. In: G. Bayle (Ed.), *L'inconscient freudien: recherche, écoute, métapsychologie* [*The Freudian Unconscious: Research, Listening, Metapsychology*] (pp. 161–170). Paris: PUF.

Donnet, J.-L. (2009). Personal communication.

Ferro, A. (2002). *In The Analyst's Consulting Room*. London: Routledge.

Freud, S. (1900a). *The Interpretation of Dreams*. S. E., 4: ix–627. London: Hogarth.

Freud, S. (1918b). *From the History of an Infantile Neurosis. S. E., 17*: 1–124. London: Hogarth.

Freud, S. (1920g). *Beyond The Pleasure Principle. S. E., 18*: 1–64. London: Hogarth.

Freud, S. (1923b). *The Ego And The Id. S. E., 19*: 1–66. London: Hogarth.

Freud, S. (1937d). Constructions in analysis. *S. E., 23*: 255–270. London: Hogarth.

Green, A. (1975). The analyst, symbolization and absence in the analytic setting (on changes in analytic practice and analytic experience). In memory of D. W. Winnicott. *International Journal of Psychoanalysis, 56*(1): 1–22.

Green, A. (2005). *Key Ideas for a Contemporary Psychoanalysis: Misrecognition and Recognition of the Unconscious*, A. Weller (Trans.). London & New York: Routledge.

Green, A. (2012). On construction in Freud's work. *International Journal of Psychoanalysis, 93*(5): 1238–1248.

Heimann, P. (1950). On counter-transference. *International Journal of Psychoanalysis, 31*: 81–84.

Levine, H. B. (Ed.) (1990). *Adult Analysis and Childhood Sexual Abuse*. Hillsdale, NJ: The Analytic Press.

Levine, H. B. (2010). Creating analysts, creating analytic patients. *International Journal of Psychoanalysis, 91*(6): 1385–1404.

Levine, H. B. (2011). Construction then and now. In: S. Lewkowicz, T. Bokanowski, & G. Pragier (Eds.), *On Freud's "Constructions in Analysis"* (pp. 87–100). London: Karnac.

Levine, H. B., Reed, G. S., & Scarfone, D. (Eds.) (2013). *Unrepresented States and the Construction of Meaning: Clinical and Theoretical Contributions*. London: Karnac.

Scarfone, D. (2011). Repetition: between presence and meaning. *Canadian Journal Psychoanalysis/Revue Canadienne de Psychanalyse, 19*(1): 70–86.

CHAPTER 9

Who is killing what or whom: some notes on the internal phenomenology of suicide

David Bell

Introduction by João Seabra Diniz

David Bell, former president of the prestigious British Psychoanalytical Society, visited Lisbon to give two exciting talks in 2015. In a pleasant and warm tone, he called for psychoanalytic debate.

In this book, we have reproduced the text that served as a basis for the workshop that has enlivened psychoanalysts and mental health professionals, who were surprised by their knowledge of the Portuguese language.

Suicide is a dramatic fact to which no one is indifferent. "Completed suicides and attempted suicides occur in the context of personality disorder". "From a psychoanalytic perspective the distinction between personality disorder and illness is in any case less clear". It is therefore a dramatic and very complex problem.

This chapter is an excellent document on the importance of psychoanalytic theory for the understanding of human functioning in general, not only for the clarity of its exposition, but also for the opportunity of its comments. At a time when there are many uses, partial or misapplied, of psychoanalytic theory, it highlights the importance of rigour in the use of concepts and procedures to be used in these cases.

Freud's initial contribution is followed by a presentation of Klein's theory.

The section entitled "The inner situation in suicide" is presented, over several pages, with rigour and clarity.

As we read, in the references it makes to "case illustrations", we can see that the author of this chapter works in a psychiatric institution. His descriptions and considerations regarding his teamwork with professionals, who do not seem to belong to the psychoanalytic community, are very useful and interesting. It is well known that this is a situation which is not rare, and is one that raises some serious issues as to the theorisation made about the cases in question and, consequently, about the various procedures to be adopted.

I quote just one sentence from his concluding comments: "attention to the relationships staff form with patients and with each other is thus critical in management".

* * *

The psychiatric literature on suicide tends to give emphasis to the demographic and social aspects. We know that completed suicide is more common in men than in women, whereas for attempted suicide the relation is reversed. Social isolation, the loss of important supporting structures which give meaning to life (such as employment and family bonds) are very important risk factors for suicide. Coming closer to the individual we know that there is a clear link between depression and suicide although there is a tendency for this to be rather overstated. It is likely that a very significant number of completed suicides and attempted suicides occur in the context of personality disorder, where, as a result of the high degree of dissociation, depressive affect is minimal. From a psychoanalytic perspective the distinction between personality disorder and illness is in any case less clear.[1]

---

[1] Illness and breakdown are viewed as developments that arise out of a particular personality structure when exposed to stress arising from internal and external sources.

Ms A, a middle-aged woman, had suffered a very significant bereavement about two years before I saw her for a consultation. She was going about her life in an apparently calm and ordinary manner, showing little outward expression of depression. She was from time to time beset by a wish, as intense as it was sudden, to hang herself. As she put it "I could be walking down the stairs having taken a break from my work to make some tea and would suddenly say to myself 'Go and hang yourself'." She kept a noose in the basement. In this case, as in many others, dissociation is a far more sinister sign than overt misery and depression.

This case brings to mind a further general feature in assessing suicide risk, namely the method that is envisaged for carrying out the act. Thoughts of overdose, for example, are usually less sinister that thoughts of self hanging or gassing.[2] The relevant feature here is, perhaps, the intensity of the internal violence that the planned method reveals.

I now put aside these general considerations, not because I believe them to be unimportant, but because they are all of limited help in understanding, assessing, and managing the individual case. The above factors lack any clear sense either of the internality of the potential suicide or of the relationship between this internality and the immediate context, particularly with reference to the most important relationships. All suicidal acts take place in the context of human relationships, real and imagined.

Freud's "mourning and melancholia"

It was consideration of those mental processes that underlie self-destruction that led Freud to a formed theory of the internal world. In 1910 the Vienna Psychoanalytic Society held a symposium on suicide and it was during that symposium that Stekel made his far-reaching remark "No-one kills himself who has never wanted to kill another, or at least wished the death of another" (1910). Freud remarked at this same

---

[2] Of course every suicide attempt needs to be taken very seriously. I remember well a patient who went to casualty having taken three paracetamol tablets which, she pointed out, was more than the recommended dose. The unwitting casualty officer told her she needn't worry as she would need to take many more to do herself any serious harm. She returned the following day having taken fifty tablets. Similarly it also pays to be wary of the patient's reassuring statement "it was all a silly mistake".

symposium that suicide would not be understood until more was known about the intricate processes of mourning and melancholia. "Mourning and melancholia" (Freud, 1917e) marked a watershed in the development of psychoanalytic theory. It was the beginning of a theory of the internal world peopled by primitive internal figures, the foundations of a theory of identification, and was also one of the crucial steps made in the development of the concept of the superego—and all of these are of course relevant to our theme. For the moment, however, I would like to examine in more detail the process of "turning against the self in hatred" which is central to Freud's paper.

Freud noted that in melancholic states the patient berated himself with various criticisms, accusations of worthlessness, weakness, etc. He suggested that, if one listened carefully to these various recriminations, one could see that they often fitted not the patient himself, but someone else who "the patient loves, has loved or should love" (Freud, 1917e, p. 248). This object of the patient's affections has been lost but instead of giving up the object the patient has dealt with his loss by incorporating the lost object into himself, identifying with it (that is, becoming it). The ego, now identified with the lost object, is now the target of all the hatred accusation that belonged originally to the object:

> The shadow of the object fell upon the ego and the latter would henceforth be judged by a special agency, as though it were an object, the forsaken object. In this way an object-loss was transformed into an ego-loss and the conflict between the ego and the loved person into a cleavage between the critical activity of the ego and the ego as altered through identification. (Freud, 1917e, p. 249)

The "critical agency" later became the superego and its activities were revealed as not just critical but archaic, cruel, and murderous. Although Freud here appears to be referring to an actual loss of a current external figure it subsequently became clear that in melancholia it is all previous losses that are activated, the losses we all have had to bear as part of development, at root the loss of the primary object, ordinarily the mother, and all that she represents. The point, however, that I wish to stress here is that underlying all suicides and similar acts of self destruction there is an attack upon the self, that is a self identified with a hated object.[3] The act is an attack upon an object and simultaneously a punishment of the self for all its sadistic and cruel attacks upon the object.

Klein's contribution

An understanding of the complexity of the internal world and the importance of states of internal persecution in mental life is central to the work of Melanie Klein. She showed how the inner world is built up through a complex interplay of processes of projection and introjection, which I now summarise.

Fundamental to development is the establishment, internally, of a good object which can be felt to support, to sustain the self in the face of the various anxiety situations that characterise development. In order to preserve the good object it is necessary for the infantile mind to create various splits, but most critical is that between his own loving and aggressive impulses. The world so formed is divided between idealised "good" objects, which are maintained internally, and "bad" ones, which are felt as persecuting and are projected externally. The more intense the infants own sadistic feelings the more terrifying the external "bad" object and the more intense the idealisation of the "good" object which is felt to offer a perfect world with absence of frustration, anxiety, or any mental pain. In this situation there is a lack of capacity to experience loss as the absence of a good object. Instead, the place where there might have been awareness of the absence of a good object is replaced by the presence of an object felt to be bad and responsible for all the painful feelings of loss and frustration.

Klein used the term "projective identification" (Klein, 1952) to describe a process, dominant in these early primitive situations, whereby internal objects and feelings are projected into objects which then become identified with that which has been projected onto them. This phase of development, dominated by these splitting and projective mechanisms, she described as the "paranoid/schizoid position". It is this inner situation that dominates in all severe psychopathology and

---

[3] "The ego can kill itself only if ... it can treat itself as an object ..." (Freud, 1917e, p. 252).

particularly so in acts of self destruction where, as I will describe further on, attempts are made to rid the self of all bad objects which have become identified with parts of the body, or even the whole self, and through so doing finally unite with an object felt to be perfect and ideal.

As infantile development proceeds the lessening of the splitting and projective processes brings a move towards integration, a process described by Klein as the move towards the depressive position. The new integration of the object brings awareness that cruel impulses have been directed towards an object that is not "just bad", but complex, not good *or* bad but good *and* bad, and this recognition brings very painful feelings of remorse and guilt and this lays the foundation for the capacity to be aware of an object which although absent remains good. This brings feelings of pining for the lost object and a mourning of its loss. The toleration of the psychic pain attendant on these processes can only be borne on the basis of the acquisition of a secure good object which provides the necessary internal support.

Klein thus described two fundamental positions, ways of being in the world. The achievement of the depressive position is not a once and for all phenomenon but is renegotiated again and again throughout life. Each developmental challenge, or traumatic situation (such as those brought by the losses that are inevitable to life) bring both the possibility of regression to illness and that of further integration. Klein thought that serious depressive illness took its point of origin at the individuals capacity to manage the psychic pain characteristic of the depressive position. It is important here to emphasise that the depressive position as defined by Klein is completely distinct from depressive illness. From the perspective offered here, depressive illness or melancholia arises from the incapacity to manage depressive pain and is characterised by primitive schizoid processes.[4]

---

[4] From a phenomenological point of view it is important to differentiate between the anxiety and psychic pain that derives from the feeling of being persecuted by an object that has been attacked, and the pain that has a more depressive quality, arising out of awareness of the damage done to the object and which mobilises reparative wishes. There is a further category, however, that appears to combine both qualities. I am referring to a particular sort of tormenting psychic pain which arises from the feeling of being internally persecuted by the recriminations of damaged objects—as if, so to speak, they are "saying" "we are all suffering, look what you have done to us". This latter situation may

It is commonly observed that patients suffering from depressive illness become dangerously suicidal when they are, in fact, recovering and this observation is quite consistent with the above account. Improvement, the move towards integration, brings the patient into touch with a persecuting guilt which it is difficult to bear. For some this results in suicidal impulses and acts as the only way of ridding the mind of the pain.

I will now describe some inner situations characteristic of suicide which will be followed by illustrating how an understanding of the inner world of the suicidal patient can influence the general management of the situation.

The inner situation in suicide

There are very few things in psychiatry that can be said with certainty and one of them is this: suicide attempts *never* take place for the stated reason. At most the cause given is the trigger and, relatively speaking, only a superficial explanation. To say, for example, that an adolescent took an overdose because he failed his exams leaves open the question as to why failing an exam results in a wish to destroy the self. A patient I knew took an overdose in adolescence, in the context of impending exams, and "exam stress" was the explanation recorded. He received no help. Later in life, when in his late forties, as a patient in analysis he was able to explain that whilst studying for his exams he was overwhelmed by the need to compulsively masturbate. His semen had left a stain that he could not eradicate and he had become terrified that his mother would "find him out". Why such a discovery terrified him, and the link between this and the conscious and less conscious fantasies that accompanied his masturbation became clear subsequently but for the present purposes this case serves to illustrate the point that what the patient recalls consciously is usually more a rationalisation than an explanation. These patients are often terrified of recognising serious mental disturbance in themselves, let alone of giving any publicity to this situation. This terror overrides the anxiety that arises from the awareness of the threat to their lives and so results in a minimisation of its seriousness.

---

lead to suicidal acts or other types of violence, motivated by the need to be rid of this type of pain which is often so unbearable.

Underlying all suicide attempts there are phantasies[5] concerning the self and the relation to the body which are usually, though not always deeply, unconscious. In addition, from a phenomenological perspective many suicide attempts occur in the context of beliefs in indestructibility. I can think of patients, for example, for whom the experience of repetitive resuscitation provided support for this omnipotence. From an internal point of view one might say, in some of these cases, a finally successful suicide, given the delusional belief in indestructibility, may be regarded as accidental.

Deep splits in the inner world between a part of the self in relation with an idealised object, and a part of the self felt to be bad and subject to terrifying inner cruel attacks, are characteristic of most suicidal patients. The idealisation serves to protect the good object from the self's own murderous wishes. The bad parts of the self may become identified with part, or even all, of the body.

I will now describe in more detail five different situations which will serve to illustrate some of the "internal phenomenologies" that underlie many suicides.

First situation. In certain patients there is a profound intolerance of frustration. Any awareness of needs or desires unsatisfied precipitates serious mental difficulties. The possibility of the awareness of absence, in line with the model described above, is replaced by the feeling of a persecuting presence often experienced as existing in the body. The body provides a particularly apt vehicle in that it is the body that brings awareness of needs and desires (such as for food, sexual contact), namely awareness of reality. Hatred of this awareness, which is critically linked to intolerance of frustration, can result in attacks on the body with the underlying phantasy that by getting rid of the body, or part of it, the patient can be rid of his desires and live on in an "ideal" world without ever having to bear again the frustration of desires unsatisfied. It is a case of "shooting the messenger", the body, because the message that it brings, awareness of painful aspects of reality, cannot be borne.

---

[5] The words phantasy is spelled here using "ph" following the convention that this spelling be used when it is unconscious phenomena that are being emphasised, distinguishing it from the more conscious events described as "fantasies".

A further aspect of these phantasies becomes apparent if one asks the question "What sort of situation in life approximates to never having to bear a need unsatisfied?" The answer is, of course, the intrauterine situation, or at least our phantasies of it. In separating himself from his hated body, the suicide may also believe that he is reuniting himself with an idealised maternal object, never to be separated again.

Second situation. The body that is attacked may represent the hated primary object, in other words an internal mother. Again there is a deep split in the mind between good and bad objects. The envied, hated mother who is attacked in phantasy is kept separate from an ideal mother felt to support life. This situation is particularly important in adolescence (see Laufer, 1995). For example, the pubertal changes in a girl's body make it increasingly difficult to locate hated sexual aspects of herself in an object, mother, that is felt to be external. Such an adolescent may experience the eruption within herself of a sexual body as evidence that she is being taken over by a hated mother. It is of interest, in this context, to recall that many who are contemplating suicide say they are prevented from carrying out the act for fear of the terrible pain it would cause to the actual parents. This, in some cases, reflects a kind of insight in that the wish to go through with the act is partly motivated by the desire to inflict this pain on the primary objects.

In all these situations "good" objects are projected outside the self and their importance should never be underestimated. A patient may say, for example, that she cannot commit suicide as long as her pet dog is alive. The dog here represents all the good objects which need to be kept alive and protected from the murderous feelings that dominate the mind.

Third situation. Klein pointed out:

> But, while in committing suicide the ego intends to murder its bad objects, in my view at the same time it also always aims at saving its loved objects, internal or external. To put it shortly: in some cases the phantasies underlying suicide aim at preserving the internalized good objects and that part of the ego which is identified with good objects, and also at destroying the other part of the ego which is identified with the bad objects and the id. Thus the ego is enabled to become united with its loved objects.
>
> (Klein, 1935, p. 160)

The point here is that, however mad it might seem, some acts of suicide are aimed at preserving what is good. It is as if the self, feeling unable to resist the pull towards terrifying destructiveness, in despair kills itself to save the world. However, it must also be true that the being lured into the belief that destruction of the self is the only way of saving the good objects might itself also be fuelled by the deadliest forces in the mind.

Fourth situation. Some suicidal patients, and this is typical of severe melancholia, are continuously internally persecuted by an archaic and vengeful superego from which there is no escape (a psychic claustrophobia).[6] Its punishing quality is merciless. It inflates quite ordinary faults and failures turning them into crimes that must be punished. In this situation suicide, a submission to the internal tormentors, may be felt as a final release. The skin itself may be felt to be the prison within which these torments take place. Cutting the skin is here associated with a feeling of relief, the self having become identified with the blood escaping. However, this relief may be overtaken by perverse excitement resulting in a frenzy of mutilating attacks. These processes also create a vicious circle in that the evidence of damage done to the objects that have become identified with parts of the body, gives fuel to further internal recriminations. It is for such a reason that some patients will go to great lengths to obtain plastic surgery to cover up their scars, which, however, can never provide what is asked of it, namely perfect, that is magical, repair all evidence of the damage inflicted being erased from the body and so from the mind.

Fifth situation. Finally I would like to address those situations where the suicidal or self-destructive act is carried out in the service of projection. Here, the patient, through the act, seeks to invade an object, projecting into it the guilt and rage he feels he has suffered at another's behest Sometimes the object of this attack is someone who has actually behaved in a cruel and tormenting way, but more often the objects only crime is to have faced the subject with unbearable "facts of life", such as the fact that he cannot control the other. Usually in such cases the subject feels that having projected the guilt, rage, and other intolerable

---

[6] Mason (1990) gives a very helpful and detailed account of this claustrophobic situation brought about by what he calls "the suffocating superego".

feelings into his object through the suicidal act, he can live on finally free of these feelings. As Alvarez (1974) has pithily put it:

> a man may take his life because he feels the destructive elements in him cannot be borne: so he sheds them at the expense of guilt and confusion of his survivors ... but what is left he hopes is a purified idealised image of himself that lives on ... suicide is simply the most brutal way of making sure you won't be forgotten.[7]

In some cases this process is further driven by an excitement borne not only of the sense of being finally rid of these bad destructive elements but also of a certain feeling of triumph over the object, believing that the object will inescapably be punished forever.

Those mental health workers who are on the receiving end of this act are left in no doubt as to the invasive power of these projective processes, not only to overwhelm one's belief in having the capacity to help that particular patient, but any patient, or even one's belief in oneself as a worthwhile human being.

Many patients describe a feeling of complete calm and peacefulness once they have resolved to kill themselves. Sylvia Plath (see Alvarez, 1974) tidied up the house, put everything in order before she gassed herself. The now tidied house confirms, symbolically, that the inner mess and confusion has been finally dealt with through the decision to commit suicide and should not be mistaken for the exercising of a balanced rational judgement. This apparent tranquillity is the outward sign that the suicide has already entered the delusional world in which he feels himself to be already free of all the inner persecution.

---

[7] Stekel makes a similar point in the symposium on suicide already referred to. He states:

> The child now wants to rob his parents of their greatest most treasured possession: his own life. The child knows that he will thereby inflict the greatest pain. Thus the punishment the child imposes upon himself is simultaneously the punishment he imposes on the instigator of his sufferings.
>
> (Stekel, [1910]1967, p. 89)

The above descriptions are not intended as a catalogue, there being a number of important situations not described here. Nor is it intended as a typology as there clearly is considerable overlap between the situations described. I have also said practically nothing about aetiology, not because it is less important—clearly factors in early childhood are of considerable importance such as childhood trauma including emotional and sexual abuse, emotional deprivation, mental illness in one or both parents—but because an accurate assessment of the inner situation is critical in rational management of these patients.

Case illustrations

Miss B was internally dominated by a cruel primitive superego which she felt watched her every move. She experienced any attempt at self control as in the service of this superego and so could not distinguish between it and ordinary ego functions that sought to protect her from danger—in other words the superego masqueraded as the ego. This resulted in a wholesale projection of her sane awareness of the danger she was in, into her analyst. She, thus left free of any concern for herself, took increasingly dangerous risks such as driving whilst under the influence of sedatives, apparently with complete equanimity, whilst her analyst became increasingly horrified as the momentum of her self-destructiveness gathered pace. She said that she experienced the ending of sessions "like a guillotine" and this was a very apt description as, having projected important ego functions into her analyst, she left the session in a "headless" state. The situation deteriorated to such an extent that it became necessary to admit her to hospital.

On the ward she behaved in a very provocative way to the nurses. She would leave the ward without telling them where she was going, leaving them with an overwhelming anxiety that she was about to carry out a very self-destructive attack. She might say, for example, in an apparently calm state, that she was "going to the shops" as if this was a quite ordinary and banal event, whilst at the same time conveying that she would be near the pharmacy where, by implication, she *might* buy some paracetamol. At other times she would telephone the ward from outside but not speak when a nurse answered and then hang up. The nurses found this unbearably tantalising. This resulted in an escalation of the need of the staff to control her and she was restricted from leaving the ward. The situation then further deteriorated and the nurses became worried that she might carry out a serious attack upon herself, at any moment. The final result was that she was restricted to a small room where she was continuously observed. She then became acutely anxious and declared in a terrified voice "I can't stand this place. I'm being imprisoned".

The patient has "actualised" (Sandler, 1976) her inner situation. What started out as an inner conflict between aspects of herself, an intrapsychic situation, has now been transported into a conflict between herself and the nursing staff, namely an interpersonal situation. The superego watching her all the time is, of course, inescapable but temporary escape is achieved through projecting it elsewhere in this way. It is not her own superego but instead the nurses on the ward who are felt to be imprisoning her.

It is also important to note that the patient's provocative manner did engender a good deal of hostility towards her which was never really owned by the staff. Although the maintenance of the patient under continuous observation served, manifestly, a wish to protect the patient from suicide, at a deeper level it also, I think, satisfied a hatred which had been recruited in the staff and which was associated with some excitement.

In the schizoid world internal good objects are felt to be under considerable threat from the subject's own murderous impulses. Some patients feel that the internal good object just cannot survive inside them and so must be projected elsewhere, in order to survive. This procedure can be lifesaving as it is through such processes that the patient recruits others to look after him. However, through a subtle shift in the balance of forces the patient can, as a result of these projective processes, become totally identified with his own cruelty, whilst the wish to live, and to secure help, becomes the target for mockery and contempt. In this perverse world strength comes only from hatred and the wish to preserve life and obtain help is regarded as evidence of weakness.

Rosenfeld (1971) gave a very detailed analysis of this process which he termed "destructive narcissism", where life-seeking parts of the personality are imprisoned and tormented by a cruel inner organisation he termed the "internal Mafia". Such patients are inexorably drawn into a perverse world where life and sanity, regarded as evidence of weakness, are treated with contempt.

Segal (1993), in discussing similar processes, gives a striking example from a literary source, Jack London's novel, *Martin Eden*. At the end of the novel, Martin, the eponymous hero, commits suicide by drowning. As he sinks, he automatically tries to swim.

> It was the automatic instinct to live. He ceased swimming, but the moment he felt water rising above his mouth his hands struck out sharply with a lifting movement. "This is the will to live", he thought and the thought was accompanied by a sneer. (Segal, 1993, p. 55)

Segal goes on:

> London brings out vividly the hatred and contempt Martin feels for the part of him that wants to live. As he drowns he has a tearing pain in his chest. "The hurt was not death" was the thought that oscillated through his reeling consciousness. It was life—the pangs of life—the awful suffocating feeling. It was the last blow life could deal him. (Segal, 1993, p. 55)

Such situations can result in a particularly deadly scenario. The patient recruits more and more people to become responsible for his own life. But the more individuals allow themselves to feel so responsible, the more the patient dissociates himself from the wish to live, now located in others. Further, as the patient becomes increasingly taken over by the cruel inner organisation, the sanity and concern now located in external others becomes the object of scorn and derision.

Ms C was referred to be considered for admission by a psychiatric team who had become very worried at the possibility of her suicide. From what I could gather threats of suicide had become one of the principle modes of communication. When I went to meet her in the waiting room she had the air of someone who was very seriously disturbed. She was sitting in the waiting room with her head bowed low and apparently did not see or hear me arrive. I had to attract her attention.

What ensued was a very disturbing experience. For much of the time she disowned any knowledge about herself claiming she had come "because they sent me". When I commented on how difficult she found the interview she replied with a defiant air, "Well anyone would in this situation, wouldn't they?".

Throughout the interview I felt acutely aware of the dangerous suicidality whilst she remained almost entirely cut off from it and apparently superior. However, when I pointed out that she was doing everything she could to stop my helping her, and went on to say that she might succeed, she looked at me, smiled and said "You've pulled the rug out from under my feet". She added that getting treatment was "her only lifeline". Although this was in a certain sense true, what I want to convey here is the way, right from the beginning of the consultation, it was I who was to carry responsibility for her condition. The waiting room situation where I had to try in a rather awkward way to attract her attention was emblematic of what was to transpire. When she said to me that getting help was her lifeline, this was not a moment of contact and reassurance. It filled me with anxiety. I felt that if I didn't accept her for treatment then and there, it would be *me* who was pulling away the lifeline, me who would be responsible for her suicide. Having projected her wish to live into me and made me responsible for it I, as the representative of that wish, was being taunted with the terror of her suicide. I carried not only the responsibility for her life but also the threat of an omnipotent persecuting guilt. The smile was a smile of perverse triumph at my impossible position. It did turn out that this was an enactment of an internal situation in which she herself felt continuously threatened and mocked. Any reference that she made to mental pain was quickly followed by a contemptuous attack on that part of herself that experienced this vulnerability labelled as "whinging and whining".

These situations are not uncommon. Many patients use admission to psychiatric wards to provide them with an immediate context for these projective procedures. Although, in the last instance, no-one can be absolutely prevented from committing suicide, it is easy for staff to become identified with an omnipotence which dictates that it is entirely their responsibility. They come to believe themselves to be the *only* ones capable of *really understanding* the patient. The determination to save the patient acquires a religiosity, the staff believing themselves to be specially selected for this mission. Hostility that is denied and split off to this extent can quite suddenly return, and with a vengeance. Yesterday's poor suffering patient who only needs help and understanding and constant support, easily becomes tomorrow's hopeless case who should be immediately discharged, given high doses of medication, or even electroconvulsive therapy. These measures may even bring an apparent improvement not based on any real development but brought about through the gratification of the patient's need for punishment, relieving him, temporarily, of the persecuting omnipotent guilt.

It was Tom Main (1957) who originally studied these processes in detail showing how the splits in the patients mind are relived, in the ward, as divisions among the staff. The "saintly" group, described above, who endlessly suffer on behalf of the patient and who believe the patient to be *only* a victim of his damaging early relationships, have their counterpart in another group of staff who see the patient *only* as manipulative and "attention seeking" which must be "confronted". Where these staff disturbances remain unacknowledged the situation can quickly escalate, with catastrophic results.

A further marked feature of these cases where perverse elements are so predominant, is the presence of negative therapeutic reactions. Here, just at the moment where the patient has made some real progress, there is a sudden deterioration with real risk of suicide. It is as if the progress with its acknowledgement of the extent of disturbance and vulnerability provokes a furious counter-attack by the internal organisation which regards this contact with sanity as a betrayal. It is important to distinguish this sort of negative therapeutic reaction from that where the pull towards suicide is primarily a result of unbearable guilt and despair, which has different management implications.

Ms D appeared, at first, as rather similar to Ms C in that she too filled the staff with unbearable anxiety as to her suicidal capacity. Although at first perverse psychopathology seemed to predominate this gave way to a more clearly melancholic picture. She had made innumerable mutilating attacks on her skin by slashing it. Her skin seemed to represent her sexual body which she regarded as disgusting. She felt full of "bad disgusting thoughts", particularly of abusing children. She felt that she could only rid herself of this identification with her abusing parent through quite literally cutting it out of her body. She had managed, however, to spare her face and hands and this appeared to represent a limited capacity to hold on to something good in herself. However, once on the ward, she tended to project into the staff all awareness of these good aspects of herself, she herself sinking further and further into a melancholic state. The fact that in this case the staff felt able to maintain a belief in her, despite being constantly provoked, turned out to be of great therapeutic importance. The primary motive for this projection outside herself of her wish to live seemed to be more for "safekeeping", perverse mockery being much less evident. After some improvement she too, like Ms C, showed a marked negative therapeutic reaction and became more acutely ill. Although there were some perverse elements the predominant difficulties arose from the unbearable psychic pain consequent on the awareness of damage done to her good objects, which to some extent really was irreparable.

Some important lessons are learnt from the management of such a case. There is a need to be constantly aware of both sides of the patient. Improvement brought an acute fear that the staff would become overexcited and so lose sight of the danger. Blindness of this type can, in some cases, precipitate further dangerous acting out as the patient needs to have her dangerousness re-registered in the minds of those responsible for her, this being a source of profound reassurance. Even when the patient was, eventually, discharged it was very important both to acknowledge the improvement, which was real, whilst accepting the ever present risk of further mutilating attacks or even suicidal attempts. These patients, I think, need to have a sense of the resilience of their object, namely an object that can bear to know of their murderousness whilst not being overwhelmed by it, nor driven to attempt to take complete control. Their needs to be a capacity to recognise the possibility of suicide without turning it into an omnipotent responsibility, thus facilitating management aimed at helping the patient rather than evading guilt. Such functions support the patient's sanity. There needs here to be a recognition that toleration of the possibility of suicide is not the same thing as colluding with it.

Institutions where these difficult patients are managed can easily themselves become vehicles for the enactment of these omnipotent processes.

At the Cassel Hospital, a regular weekly meeting of all the staff aims to discuss difficulties in the work, regardless of source. In the first meeting after a suicide had taken place, the staff were understandably stunned, especially as the patient was not thought to be in such immediate danger. During the meeting one of the staff reminded those present that the staff in the previous week's meeting had spent much of the meeting discussing the nurses re-grading. This referred to the implementation of a new NHS policy which required all qualified nurses to be re-graded. This meant that nurses who were at the same level in the hierarchy would, within a few days, find that some of them were now on a higher grade and thus receiving more money. This had been a considerable source of stress for the nurses and was interfering with their work. The meeting, at the time, was largely felt to have been useful. However, with the knowledge now at hand, it was asserted that this discussion had "really" been a defensive distraction from anxiety concerning the patient who had killed herself. Soon there emerged the implication that if we had talked about the patient we would have saved her life. The meeting ended in an atmosphere of guilt and recrimination.

The following week, as I walked down the corridor to the meeting, I suddenly found myself wanting to use the meeting to talk about any patient under my care who was suicidal. I then remembered that it is often the patient who one is not particularly worried about who actually commits suicide. So the category "suicidal" widened its reference until it included all the patents under my care. I then felt impelled to discuss all of them in the meeting. Others wanted to discuss their patients. It became evident that the wish to discuss patients was no longer in any realistic relation to a wish to improve their care but was now at the service of a wish to escape blame from an omnipotent organisation which, in the event of a suicide, would hold staff completely responsible and ensure they were punished.

Concluding comments

In this chapter I have firstly drawn attention to the different internal phenomenologies that underlie attacks upon the self. I have tried to show how an understanding of the patient's inner world can be an essential part of management. Inner situations can be externalised in various ways resulting in quite irrational management based more on countertransference enactments than sober consideration of the issues. A particularly dangerous situation is where the patient succeeds, through projective processes, in externalising his inner world to such an extent that external objects become indistinguishable from archaic inner figures making reality testing impossible.

Attention to the relationships staff form with patients and with each other is thus critical in management. We all enter the field of mental health for complex reasons but probably common to us all is a wish to repair our own damaged inner objects. In order to be able to work effectively we need to be able to tolerate the patient's attacks on these reparative wishes, our most vulnerable point. We need to be able to stand failure so that the patient can improve for himself rather than experiencing the need for progress as a demand from those caring for him.

More than anything else staff morale is the vital therapeutic ingredient, a morale that needs to be robust and not dependent on any individual patient getting better. I have described a common central structure in suicidal patients, a primitive psychotic superego which demands omnipotence, not knowledge. It is easy for such disturbed modes of thinking to find a home not only in the staff but in the institution itself especially when this is backed up by an external world that demands the impossible. Insisting that mental health personnel accept a level of responsibility that is quite unrealistic seems increasingly to be a part of mental health policy. Such policies based less on thought and more on the wish to project unmanageable anxiety into those faced with an already very difficult task, set the scene for a deterioration in the real care of these patients. Management plans come to serve to defend the self against any possible blame rather than acceptance of the complexities of the task. An attitude of enquiry is transformed into protecting oneself from the inquisition.

References

Alvarez, A. (1974). *The Savage God: A Study of Suicide*. Harmondsworth, Middlesex: Penguin.

Freud, S. (1917e). Mourning and melancholia. *S. E., 14*: 237–258. London: Hogarth.

Klein, M. (1935). A contribution to the psychogenesis of manic-depressive states. *International Journal of Psychoanalysis*, 16: 145–174.

Klein, M. (1952). Notes on some schizoid mechanisms. In: M. Klein, P. Heimann, S. Isaacs, & J. Riviere (Eds.), *Developments in Psychoanalysis* (pp. 292–320). London: Routledge, 1989.

Laufer, M. (Ed.) (1995). *The Suicidal Adolescent*. London: Karnac.

Main, T. F. (1957). The ailment. *British Journal of Medical Psychology*, 30(3): 129–145.

Mason A. (1990). The suffocating super-ego: psychotic break and claustrophobia. In: J. S. Grotstein (Ed.), *Do I Dare Disturb the Universe? A Memorial to W. R. Bion* (pp. 139–166). London: Karnac.

Rosenfeld, H. (1971). A clinical approach to the psychoanalytical theory of the life and death instincts: an investigation into the aggressive aspects of narcissism. *International Journal of Psychoanalysis*, 52(2): 169–178.

Sandler, J. (1976). Countertransference and role-responsiveness. *International Review of Psychoanalysis*, 3: 343–347.

Segal, H. (1993). On the clinical usefulness of the concept of death instinct. *International Journal of Psychoanalysis*, 74(1): 55–61.

Stekel, W. ([1910]1967). Symposium on suicide. In: P. Friedman (Ed.), *On Suicide: With Particular Reference to Suicide Among Young Students* (pp. 33–141). New York: International Universities Press.

CHAPTER 10

Achieving the elasticity of technique: Sándor Ferenczi's psychoanalytic project and journey*

Franco Borgogno

Introduction by Rui Aragão Oliveira

Franco Borgogno, a psychoanalyst at the Italian Psychoanalytical Society, is known for promoting intense debate between psychoanalysis and academia (he was chair of the International Psychoanalytical Association's Psychoanalysis and University Committee). It was for this exact reason that he first visited Lisbon, enchanting many of his Portuguese colleagues with his enthusiasm and profound knowledge, and immediately sparking intense discussion.

As a spontaneous reaction, a small group of Portuguese psychoanalytical colleagues took it upon themselves to promote his return in 2012, this time with the purpose of reflecting on the work of Sándor

* Paper presented at the S. Ferenczi International Conference of Budapest titled "Faces of trauma" on 1 June 2012. A slightly different version of it was read in Madrid on 7 March 1997 at the International Congress on "Ferenczi and contemporary psychoanalysis", and then published in 2001 in *The American Journal of Psychoanalysis* (61(4): 391–407). I wish to thank *The American Journal of Psychoanalysis* for having granted permission to publish it in the present form in this book.

Ferenczi and its historical importance, in a contemporary view of psychoanalysis. Contact with one of the most important authors of psychoanalysis, close to Freud, with whom he maintained a scientific dialogue of enormous richness and scope, triggered a unique interest and reflection. Franco Borgogno was able to capture this attention on Ferenczi's contributions, promoting further contact with Luis Martín Cabré, Judit Mészáros, and Anette Blaya Luz, who, in later visits, also shared their Ferenczian knowledge with the group.

These communications were decisive in "restoring" the texts of Sándor Ferenczi to the training of Portuguese psychoanalysts. They are now studied regularly, which facilitates the frequent collaboration of several of our colleagues with the International Sándor Ferenczi Network.

In this already historic text, despite being written some years ago—as mentioned in the Postscript section and which was also reproduced in the Portuguese psychoanalytical review, *Revista Portuguesa de Psicanálise*—Franco Borgogno presents to us not only the innovation introduced by Ferenczi with the "elasticity of technique", but also a very current issue concerning the identity problem of the analyst, and the assumption of the responsibility that they should inevitably assume as a permanent challenge in the exercise of their clinical activity.

* * *

The "elasticity of technique" which Ferenczi proposed in his 1928 study of that title does not simply mark a particular phase in his psychoanalytic experimentation, nor can it be seen as his point of arrival (Ferenczi, 1928a). Those with an intimate knowledge of Ferenczi's thought will recognise it rather as a *profound dimension of a general psychoanalytic attitude* which gradually fermented and matured across his experience, coming to produce substantial changes in his theory and practice.

In this chapter I intend to give a brief outline of the *psychic conditions and values* which constituted the foundation of this attitude, psychic conditions, and values that have progressively made Ferenczi's contribution to psychoanalysis amazingly modern and appealing for new generations of psychoanalysts. They are the following: (1) the authority which he gained through his practical experience in the field; (2) his unqualified willingness to put himself on the line; (3) his special capacity for imaginative-elaborative identification with the patient's emotions and thoughts, and, in particular, with his legitimate needs and expectations (a capacity accompanied by compassion and respect). Ferenczi indicated these three characteristics, which could be broadly subsumed under the experience he called "feeling at one with" (*Einfühlung*), as being idiosyncratically elective of "being a psychoanalyst" to a community of colleagues who at the time were not yet fully ready to accept them and to really take them on board.

For Ferenczi, elasticity did not mean, as many still claimed (even Freud, in some way), indulgence and symmetry, but essentially *the starting point for the analyst to acknowledge and work-through his own influence and functions in the analytic process, his own limitations included*. The implication—and this is the point I would like to stress—was a *heightened responsibility and responsiveness* of the analyst in his daily reception of the patient along with a greater awareness of the elements of subjectivity involved in his participation both in each session and in the "longer-term wave" of an analysis. Every analysis in fact, even if it appears in the guise of a scientific method and professional routine, can itself—in his view—contribute to the repetitive and "massifying" structuring of the encounter (Ferenczi, 1925, p. 271) through obedience to the unreflected group basic assumptions linked to conformism and to an anti-developmental unconscious collusion.

Obviously, Ferenczi himself did not have complete access to the tools required to attain this ideal; nonetheless the clinical issues inherent to his analytical position became clearer and clearer to him and, with time, to the majority of us.

The project and its debut

From the viewpoint I wish to adopt here, which principally sees *elasticity of technique as a never-ending journey in Ferenczi's life and work*, the first steps towards the realisation of this ideal are the observations contained in his pre-analytic writings, 1899 to 1908 (Mészáros, 1999). In these works, the young Ferenczi, who had not yet encountered Freud, anticipated and made explicit the values that became fundamental to his future therapeutic practice. He questioned the medicine and psychiatry of his day and denounced what he saw as *aspects of knowledge and power* that revealed its practitioners to be inherently conceited and lax in their care for patients and for patients' suffering. In other words, he denounced the fact that, in substance, practitioners could too easily lose sensitivity, solidarity, and sincere interest in the pain and needs of their patients, which instead should have been at the centre of their attention and listening, and equally too easily and rapidly forget and conceal their mistakes and limits under a falsely superior and idealising stance, founded on a denial of ignorance and of the fallibility of one's own means, while these, if recognised and accepted, were for Ferenczi the privileged heuristic instruments to extend understanding and competence (see, as an example and testimony of this epistemophilic and mental posture, his 1906 translation of a "Letter from G-A Dumas to a young person intending to study medicine" (Lorin & Almassy, 1983), and his brief 1903 review "Where memory sleeps").

Indeed, right from the start Ferenczi's critical work in the field of psychoanalysis had, as its primary objective, the challenge to the provisional and transient nature of knowledge, the misery of human attitudes, and the overestimation of one's own abilities and perspectives, a challenge quite explicit in the Freud–Ferenczi correspondence (Freud & Ferenczi, 1908–1933). Over the course of this correspondence, Ferenczi, through his rapport and dialogue with Freud (Haynal, 2001), bombarded his colleagues, Freud, and of course himself with an interminable series of questions that, so to speak, "put at issue" the young and as yet uncertain basic psychoanalytic principles, but did so without any nihilism. He rather wanted to temper the noble fibre of the psychoanalytic method in order *to better adapt it to the psychic lacks of patients and not to allow it to lapse in the face of difficulty into non-thought and fatalism.*

To state the matter differently, Ferenczi put the "obvious" "to work", considering it as an important source of the dissociated and repressed unconscious. Among the "obviousnesses" that were to come under his scrutiny were those *dimensions, functions, and mental operations* that, insofar as they serve to ground psychic life and our understanding of it, themselves become automatic[1] and for this reason are no longer

---

[1] Ferenczi's work on the "automatism of thought" is considerable: see his study on its origins in the suggestive and hypnotic elements of the relationship (Ferenczi, 1908c, 1909, 1913a, 1913b, 1920–1932, 1924a, 1924b); his underlining of the children's acceptance of

observed, reflected on, discussed, and mentioned. What Ferenczi essentially had in mind, in this regard, was those behaviours of a routine or ordinary nature which are generally deemed normal and granted, and even useful, while they may turn out to be quite the reverse. They may, in fact, harbour—as Ferenczi demonstrated (chiefly in his *The Clinical Diary*, 1932b)—*aspects of an abuse (of power) and a devious and subtle violence, which not rarely serve to mask a laziness, insensitivity, indifference, and ambiguity that show little respect for either the patient or the psychoanalytic method itself.*

In this connection, we should also recall at this point that Ferenczi's goal was to expand on Freud's concept of the unconscious, including in it that which never became mentally inscribed and that which remained unspoken in the patient's infancy and past, frequently on account of inadequate nurturing and education (Borgogno, 2002). To his mind, in short, the "obvious" represented an area in which are deposited countless uncertainties, doubts, profound anxieties, and mysteries that the exploring mind cannot bear since these would be too disturbing if removed from the silence that envelops them—that realm of the unsaid often imposed, interdicted, and sanctioned by the community itself.

As soon as Ferenczi, the "*enfant terrible* of psychoanalysis", arrived on the scene, he to all intents and purposes brought into play and disrupted the secure mental base of both parents and masters tirelessly investigating how knowledge in analysis arises, how it is reached, and how it is transmitted. And, in proceeding through this line of inquiry (that is, considering which particular values, feelings, and responses guide, facilitate, or impede the analytic conversation and the subjectivation of the patient), he started to pay close attention to *the place assigned to the "other" and his specificity in the course of coupling*, a coupling that Ferenczi wished to make quite mutually profitable and satisfying, and not at all inappropriate or traumatic.

---

physical and mental violence since they consider these to be normal and habitual aspects of their life context, and also because—on account of the unbearable nature of suffering—they are no longer conscious of such violence (Ferenczi, 1931, 1932a, 1932b); his repeated exhortation that the analysis should privilege the patient's point of view and his capacity for self-representation (Ferenczi, 1929, 1931).

To put it another way, just like the intelligent, curious, and at the same time highly sensitive and vulnerable child he came to describe, Ferenczi was not interested in knowing purely how one is born or how one grows as a person (patient or analyst). His focus, on the contrary, was on investigating *the dynamics and objectives of any encounter between two minds*, questioning *the quality* and *rhythm of their exchange as well as the pleasure or displeasure* each member of the couple feels. Hence, he did not settle for mere factual information—which is always external—about what he calls the "botanical" aspects of "mental coition" (Ferenczi, 1908c, p. 281; 1927a, pp. 69–71): he was aiming at something much more intimate and profound which has to do with the libidinal and affective characteristics that generate meaning and significance within the relationship. "Gardening of the soul" ("horticulture", Ferenczi, 1908c, p. 281) and "obstetric propensity" (Ferenczi, 1919a, p. 182)—these were some of Ferenczi's evocative metaphors to outline the analyst's ability to intuitively individuate that what his patient mainly desires is not a correct explanation but to feel "how" the analyst has himself passed through the turbulence and the emotional crisis similar to that being experienced by the patient as a part of the act of arriving at the interpretation.[2]

Suffice to recall here that this theme—the origin and nature of psychological understanding—was to be the very subject of Ferenczi's opening remarks in the 1928 paper that I am discussing. However, the theme of efficient coupling, its fruits and disturbances, was—as I have underlined (Borgogno, 1999a, 1999b)[3]—also the subject of Ferenczi's

---

[2] Bion himself was to take on this idea in the 1970s (Bion, 1992; Borgogno & Merciai, 2000).

[3] This brief paper of 1908, without any doubt, is a true "calling card" that metaphorically points to what, to my mind, will be the horizons and later direction of his discourse on technique: the search for more democratic and synchronic emotional conditions both during the "foreplay" of an analysis that creates the basis for the relation between patient and analyst and in the mental actions through which the analysis is consummated and made both vital and creative; the emphasis on the patient's verbal and non-verbal responses to the behaviour, phantasies, and feelings shown by the analyst during the session, since these are often unreceptive and untransformative on account of their being inconstant if not masturbatory and precociously ejaculative; and finally the preparation of a relational and thinking space which is there to invite the weaker, disadvantaged "other" to take part in the analysis as a full partner whose voice initially needs to be

first psychoanalytic paper of 1908, "The effect on women of premature ejaculation in men" (1908a), where, in a way that was highly original for its time, he studied premature ejaculation on the basis of its effects on women, taking on a strongly relational perspective in emphasising the relevance of the rhythm and tempo of the encounter, and giving particular weight to the specific idiosyncrasies of the partner. This latter constitutes a research approach that Ferenczi had already anticipated in 1902 in the surprising treatment of Rosa K (Ferenczi, 1899–1908, in Mészáros, 1999), a woman who felt herself to be a man, when he had asked the patient to write down her life history on the grounds that this was a case where the psychiatrist would certainly know less about her transvestite condition than she knew herself.

Showing *respect* for, and *safeguarding, the voice of the "other" (first and foremost, the voice of the infant and child)* were, therefore, from the onset crucial values for Ferenczi, and this is particularly evident if we are to follow his way of thinking through the wealth of observations he made regarding "trauma" and "the traumatic" in all his writings. Indeed, a significant "red thread" runs across many of the histories of neglected children that lie behind Ferenczi's first cases: the little boy who, during an operation for hydrocele, suddenly found his mouth covered with a chloroform mask (1929); the little girl whose father, a smoker, put his tongue between her lips whenever he kissed her (1908b); the boy whose mother could not bear it when his voice broke because she perceived its full and sonorous masculine bass tonality as a sign of his dawning manhood and an incestuous fixation that would be dangerous for her (1915). This same "red thread" is connected with the analysis style of his mature period when, having concentrated his reflection on the traumatic situations, he became especially careful—albeit with obvious deficiencies—*not to introduce words and feelings that would be alien or foreign to the heart, mouth or mind of the "other"*. This is the clinical approach on which I am focusing and which made Ferenczi the natural precursor of many psychoanalysts belonging to the British Independent School (Borgogno, 1995) and to the American Relational Trend (Berman, 1998).

---

supported, awakened, and tutored by a process that seeks to come to know this voice and thus restore it to greater human dignity.

To sum up, in Ferenczi's project, it was the discovery, appreciation, and protection of alterity that provided the key to his approach towards, and centred on, the patient in the exploration of the unconscious, that unconscious which Freud had posited as the cornerstone of psychoanalysis. This exploration, as Ferenczi would continue to suggest throughout his analytical journey, could not be reduced to either the endorsement of a given form of "acritical and mimetic identification" with the aggressor, or a sort of "suggestively hypnotic submission to a fetish". It is precisely in this area—as Ferenczi made clear in the conclusion to his 1928 essay—that the analyst must be on his guard, since here, more than anywhere else, lurks one of the greatest perils for an analysis: the danger of a "slavish obedience" to the unconscious, parasitic, and narcissistic components of the superego (Ferenczi, 1928a, p. 101). Right at this juncture, for Ferenczi, lies that insidious trap which, demanding that mobility of the libido be renounced and the consequent sacrifice of the future potential "becoming" of the two subjects involved, kills the very dialogue that the analysis seeks to promote and realise intra- and inter-psychically.

The journey and the model

For the reasons I have just stated, Ferenczi, more than any other psychoanalytic pioneer, personifies the essence of psychoanalysis as an *authentic exercise of thought and sensitivity placed at the service of the patient and the understanding of his suffering*, so much so that the famous observation by Granoff "if Freud invented psychoanalysis, it was Ferenczi who embodied it" (Granoff, 1958, p. 85) seems entirely appropriate.

From his early *sorties* as an analyst, in fact, psychoanalysis for Ferenczi was not the somewhat rational and cognitive activity of transmitting knowledge about the unconscious, as it often proved to be in his time, but above all a *live experience: one that comes from the heart and is rooted in an affective relationship and dialogue, upon which reflection proceeds by trial and error*. Starting from this ardent "conviction"[4] he

---

[4] The idea of the analyst's "conviction" is one of Ferenczi's "hobby horses" that he would continue to pursue throughout his oeuvre. His thinking in this regard is perhaps best

effectively was to introduce an innovative praxis foreshadowing a future *paradigm change* that shifted the accent of the analysis *from a more distancing and objective gaze focused on verbal material to the study of the intersubjective–communicative interaction between transference and countertransference*, both in the "here and now" of the session and in the unfolding of a psychoanalysis.

By undertaking such a change in technique he would, of course, come to reject the inevitable pedagogical, philosophical, and religious appeal, undeniably at work when the analyst approaches the treatment with an excessively strong and well-defined theory, and would, as a consequence, increasingly opt for the notion of *an emotional test and momentary suspension of judgement, filtered and reinforced by his working-through of the patient's resonance on him, as its chosen means of encounter and instrument of understanding.*

Although this orientation taken by Ferenczi may—at a first glance—seem somewhat more provisional, it was in reality much more daring and complex and, in his view, the psychoanalytic route *par excellence*, the route that can *realise the evenly-suspended attention* recommended by Freud and *recompose "the dissociation of sensibility"* which is at the root of mental distress (Ferenczi, 1919a).[5] Moreover, in his opinion, this was the best way of overcoming the often arid and restrictive limits of language and representation; that is to say: a means to truly contain that which defies thought.

For Ferenczi, in practise, the first moment of knowledge requires that the analyst identify with, and lose himself in, the "other"—in the

---

summed up in the paper he delivered in Madrid in 1928 entitled "The training of the psychoanalyst": "A form of knowledge ... which in us becomes conviction only through our own experience, that is, through the analysis of ourselves" (1928b) p. 341.

[5] This is the area of pathology that Ferenczi deals with in his psychoanalytic work both with neurotics and, above all, with those difficult patients on whom he would become a "specialist": patients who "experience intense sensations and emotions though they do not associate"; or who "freely associate though they do not feel"; who "perhaps speak with acute perceptive capacity about themselves and others, but cannot really see themselves or those they talk about on a conscious level"; who "do not know how to talk about what they feel in any way meaningful for themselves" and "do not know from where and how these feelings come about".

relationship. It is exclusively by temporarily *forgoing the idealisation of consciousness in favour of unquestioningly exposing himself to all the unconscious libidinal movements necessary to sustain a relationship* that he can really enter into contact with the singularity of any relationship and slowly become able to put it into words that have authentic significance in the present.[6] Solely in this way might he concretely, *without wishing to possess them a priori, play host and give a name to the myriad messages that the two unconsciouses send each other.* As a consequence, we could say that it was Ferenczi's major task to reconnect—guided by the variable and unpredictable lengths of time that the messages require—both with the vital elementary needs and universal desires that foster them and with the objects to which the messages are imaginarily addressed.[7]

In this conception of the psychoanalytic process as primarily a *two-way exchange of lived experience and unconscious communications*, we can see Ferenczi in tune with the Freud who theorised the dialogue of the unconscious (Freud, 1912), but an equally valid model of reference would be the Freud of the period I like to call that of "Little Hans and his surroundings".[8] I have in mind here the Freud of "On

---

[6] In order to enter into real contact with the singularity of their patients, analysts need to be open to receive the various roles progressively assigned to them in the course of the analytic treatments; in short, during the analyses, they must regress as their patients do, and in their stead, consenting to temporarily "interpret" all those aspects of the patients' self and internal objects which—in order to survive the traumatic experiences encountered in life—have been dissociated by the patients themselves (see Borgogno, 2007, 2008, 2011; Borgogno & Vigna-Taglianti, 2012).

[7] Here it should be stressed that Ferenczi is already foreshadowing the differentiation between "survival needs of the ego" and "drive-based desires". Balint and Winnicott will further expand this difference, distinguishing between classical neurotic pathology and borderline–psychotic pathology. Anna Freud and American psychoanalysis were later to develop this very point using the terms "developmental arrest" and "delays".

[8] Here I refer to the Freud who had a profound knowledge of infantile states of mind and who, during this period (1905–1908), was particularly sensitive to children's points of view. For example, when he wrote that their capacity to respond with intelligence, curiosity, and great openness to life and novelty can be smothered by the evasive reticence, hypocrisy, and lack of interest of adults (Freud, 1908, 1909); or when he argued that their highly suggestible nature does not make them abandon the pursuit of truth, which they still do in a hidden or split off way; or again, when he recalled that oedipal children inevitably feel guilty about something (Freud, 1906) and thus may easily be accused of just about anything; and when he stressed the need to distinguish their compliance—occasioned by

psychotherapy" (1904), when, in his attempt to claim a place for psychoanalysis among the sciences, he first endorses the self-restraint of the analyst that operates *"per via di levare"* and not *"per via di porre"*, and then preconsciously offers the floor to Shakespeare's Hamlet, who shows how only through the heart—or rather, by being sincerely and profoundly open within a relationship—can we meet the "mystery of another person's heart". This is, evidently, the same Freud who only a few years later, now in his capacity as a supervisor of Little Hans and his father, was able—also thanks to his own self-analysis—to begin to take "a second look" at his work and give a greater help to the working couple (Freud, 1909), assuming both a more measured and fruitful distance from his early—overpowering and colonising—passion for theory and interpretation, and a consequent closer contact with the sensitive, intelligent, preconscious responses that the child in the patient signalled to him.

This model, on the grounds of which *knowledge is in transit and the subject of discourse partly unfolds unbeknown to the two partners that form the relationship* (that is, to the analyst too), was exactly, in my view, the core of Ferenczi's first technical paper: "On transitory symptom-constructions during the analysis" (1912a). In this paper—which has gone almost unremarked in the rich contemporary literature on his thought—if Ferenczi brought to light, besides to the importance of the verbal language, that of *the* "discourse of the body" when the more desirable verbal route to awareness is not available (thus anticipating as many have noted the writings of Groddeck and W. Reich), he really did much more than that: he noted *the effect of the analyst's silences and words on the other*, and stressed that the patient's reaction is indicative not merely of his affective particular mode of listening but of the quality of the participation of the analyst as well.

Ferenczi, in other words, started from here in putting forward useful amendments to the analytic process. On the one hand—prefiguring, for example, the Rosenfeld of *Impasse and Interpretation* (1987), the Ferro of *The Bi-personal Field* (1992) and, in a sense, the Faimberg of

---

helplessness and intense need—from falsity or intentional and inveterate lying. It is self-evident that this is the version of Freud that Ferenczi will make use of and take further in his own work, by exploring the context within which the mind develops and transforms.

the "Listening to listening" (1996)—he understood *the pre-verbal,
verbal, and non-verbal responses of the patient to be a secret, hidden
and sometimes dissociated comment on the attitudes and mental functioning expressed by the analyst* at a given moment in the session and in
the analytic relationship (see also Ferenczi, 1913c, 1919a, 1921, 1929).
On the other hand—being particularly able to accept to "live through"
and be surprised by the "other" that is inside himself no less than inside
the patient (Borgogno, 2011)—he even came to broach the realm of
projective identifications later to be discovered by his student, Melanie
Klein (1946), and subsequently explored by Bion (an analysand of Klein
previously analysed by Rickman, another of Ferenczi's students and
fervent supporters).

Being, in this decidedly open and unwearied position, inspired to
pursue a more attentive and more humble form of listening—and on this
matter he differs from the most rigid and dogmatic aspects of Klein and
of the Kleinians (at least those of the first generation)—the analyst for
Ferenczi must be willing to "abdicate" power and knowledge in their most
arrogant manifestations, since his understanding and interpretations,
not necessarily "at target", could, on the contrary, present errors,
with the effect of constraining and inhibiting growth. But errors and
deficits—he added—even when they are signs of some kind of failure,[9]
are at the same time potential *means to knowledge* and *an occasion for
re-opening and re-transcribing the past*, providing that the analyst can
accept being "found out" by them, generously harbouring an "otherness
in the making" that he must not erase in the daily process of analysing
it. This is a point of view that Winnicott, undoubtedly impressed by the
works of Ferenczi and the Balints (Borgogno, 2006), carried forward and
which today has been broadly theorised in the United States using the
notion of *enactment* (Jacobs, 1986; Ogden, 2001).

---

[9] The difference between Ferenczi and Melanie Klein in this respect is very well expressed
in Ferenczi's answer to a question of Klein's at the London conference of 1927. When
Klein asked him to explain how to teach children symbolism and the use of symbols,
he replied: "We should in general learn symbols from children rather than they from
us", and that "symbols are the language of children; they have not to be taught how to
understand them. They have only to feel the other person has the same understanding of them that they themselves have when acceptance becomes immediate" (Ferenczi,
1927a, p. 76).

To recapitulate the stretch of the journey I have been illustrating thus far, Ferenczi aimed to temper the narcissism and surreptitious suggestiveness lurking behind the analyst's attempt to carry out his function and, in line with his new sensitivity towards the patient's responses to interpretation and to the deeply rooted ways of being of the analyst during the session, he began to vigorously check for, and root out, signs of "belief" or "disbelief" towards analysis (1913b)[10] giving gradually more value to the patient's criticisms, the "larval" forms (Ferenczi, 1919a, 1919b, 1919c) in which these appeared, often concealed beneath gestures of acquiescence and submission (Ferenczi, 1926; Ferenczi & Rank, 1924). In so doing, Ferenczi would explicitly come to consider himself as a vitally *important, albeit fallible and limited, "life remain"*: implicated in the intra-/inter-psychic events that his patients reported, which were in part always potentially linked to some element in the analyst himself. Extraordinarily illuminating and incisive in this regard are the numerous observations he would subsequently make on *the acuteness of patients' perceptiveness* and on their *indispensable contribution to the development of interpretation and working-through*,[11] even when such a contribution is commonly labelled "resistance".

---

[10] Ferenczi's work is commonly considered wanting in terms of his analysis of patients' negative responses, yet he is in reality a pioneer in this area. However, for him, the working-through of the negative transference is always linked to the patient's contribution to the analyst's self-analysis (Ferenczi, 1920–1932, 1927b, 1928a, 1932b). He is consequently highly attentive to hostile and non-constructive behaviour. In the process of understanding the patient's projective identifications and the role-reversals that characterise the analytic impasse, however he is inclined (because of his own personal problems) to overly absolve the patient, taking upon himself more than is necessary and feeling he must resolve the patient's difficulties whatever the cost. His conception of destructiveness as reactive to the various kinds of environmental deprivation led him to place at the centre of the analysis not the reparation of the object, hypothetically damaged by the patient, but rather the "reconstruction of an incomplete and as yet unborn self", due to parental inadequacies. Furthermore, it is not true that Ferenczi was unaware of the improper aspects of his excessive tendency towards reparation. Indeed, he discovered two fundamental concepts in this context: the well-known concept of the "wise baby" and that of "terrorism of suffering", lucidly revealing the complex double bind that comes with them. He was continuing to work on these ideas when he died in 1933 (Borgogno, 1999a, 2011).

[11] The notion of working-through was central to Ferenczi's work, as he himself declared (1927b). See also "Suggestion and psycho-analysis" (1912b) for an idea of the subtlety of Ferenczi's thinking on this point.

Moreover, Ferenczi's wish to verify personally (in the manner of a latter-day Aquinas), and from case to case, the validity of the Freudian concepts and technical procedures, was his peculiar way *to call into play*—admittedly with some ingenuousness and a certain discontinuity in his conduct—*the point of view of the patient,*[12] *activating and reawakening him to non-alienated mental life* (this was the real meaning of his "active technique"), also when neither patient nor analyst fully possessed the instruments to reach this objective. While such research—considered by many obscure if not "deviant"—was surely excessive, for Ferenczi it was a mandatory step for moderating presumption and arrogance, as well as avoiding consecrating one's own preconceptions and prejudices in the pursuit of truth. Therefore, we could say today that, if Ferenczi erred, it was in the poetic and etymological sense of the word: he left the beaten track of tradition, in order *not to elude those questions that would enable knowledge to progress* and also to nourish and alert our authentic epistemophilic movement towards its shadow zone.

In brief, throughout his life, Ferenczi's work is *a model of psychoanalytic commitment* and a career-long homage to our discipline and to its founder. As he explored and adopted technical modifications, he always *tried to learn from experience*—an attitude which culminated in his inaugurating what he calls in *the elasticity of technique* "a metapsychology of the analyst's mental processes during analysis" (1928a, p. 98). In effect, what he there proposed was that we *reflect on the active components involved in the analyst's communications and non-communications*, since these are ineluctably unconscious manifestations that surpass even the best intentions of *abstinence* and neutrality. In this sense, Ferenczi dedicated all his passion and enthusiasm *to seeking out the origins of transformation experimentally and, in particular, those which are still missing, still to come (what is "to come"*, as he wrote), and this is what may be, or may become the future subject of knowledge, since it is we

---

[12] Paula Heimann, Michael and Alice Balint, Margaret Little, Winnicott, and Bollas follow Ferenczi in his "celebration of the patient", which, beyond the high-flown term, means: respecting the patient's qualities and creativity, which, along with all his various other aspects, must be put into words during the analysis and, if necessary, openly recognised and validated.

analysts who have authorised ourselves to embody it and who are the first to encounter it.

Conclusions

"What does Ferenczi mean by 'elasticity of technique'?", then, the reader might well still ask. The answer is given by Ferenczi himself, who borrows a felicitous metaphor from one of his patients in his 1928 paper on elasticity. It involves *remaining* at one end of an "elastic band" *in complete contact with the patient*, as we have been and may continue to be, in the analytic encounter, *but resolute*—as regards to the functions required of us and for consistency's sake—*in our role as depository and receiver both of his symbolic destiny* as a subject and of *his hopes and fears* for the future.[13] We must be *companions in our participation* (in the sense of participating "with" but also "towards", and if necessary, "in place of" the patient)[14]—Ferenczi adds—*to help the patient transform his anxieties, conflicts and traumas* into something thinkable: something that could be linked to one's personal history[15] and so be integrated into an affectively vital identity that heralds more effective existential options and more practicable and fitting life solutions. At the end, this is the kind of transformation which, for Ferenczi, can make the patients no longer uncritically dependent on the internal and external world and better able to

---

[13] For Fédida (1992) a noticeable virtue of Ferenczi's work lies in the way it links the particularity of an individual destiny with a knowledge of universal events that are emotionally close to us all and which constitute that "all" without which all singularity would descend into nothingness.

[14] Here I refer above all to the "auxiliary" ego functions that are necessary in the treatment of highly disturbed patients; but, for Ferenczi, as for Heimann (see Borgogno, 1999a, 1999b), an analyst who does not work *per via di porre* is unthinkable.

[15] In this chapter I have touched upon the intersubjective and communicational modernity of Ferenczi's technique. In his view, however, the "here and now" and the present relationship were to be worked-through both in connection with the patient's past and his/her particular history, and with his/her internal world. The analysis, above all, must not sacrifice historical material and it is for this that he was highly critical of Rank (Ferenczi, 1926), who did not consider such material useful and tended to take a strongly relational perspective; in Ferenczi's view what Rank proposed was a caricature of the essence of analysis. Faimberg's idea of "listening to listening" (1996) can be traced back to Ferenczi.

discriminate phantasy from reality, self from other, and, when required, to separate themselves from the devastatingly harmful effects caused by objects, which in the past were of little use in really tutoring them in terms of their own specificity.

To conclude: with his concept of "elasticity of technique", Ferenczi pioneered an analytical approach whose ultimate goal was to *render the patient less permeable to the archaic and unwitting valencies of incorporation and introjection* (Borgogno, 2009). He did this first of all by, loyally and synergistically (with that imaginative and elaborative identification which was for him "tact"), encouraging and sustaining the development of the *capacity to barricade oneself against invasions (a "no-entry" capacity),* preventing "the other" from displaying the kind of affectivity whereby the latter imposes his own heterogeneous needs, feelings, anxieties, and inappropriate mentalities and ideologies. This is a healthy defence mechanism, which present-day and future analysts who *"ally themselves with psychic life"* may contribute towards constructing as an anti-traumatic barrier not only against possible attempts at intrusion or projection but also against the extrajection of aspects of the self which, instead, may flourish, as long as they are confirmed and validated, or which are awaiting a new possibility to be born (Balint, 1968; Bollas, 1987, 1989; Borgogno, 1997; Heimann, 1989).

Postscript

Even though this paper was written more than twenty years ago and presented for the first time at the 1997 International Sándor Ferenczi Congress on "Ferenczi and contemporary psychoanalysis" in Madrid, I would not change a single comma today. It was my calling card to the Ferenczian world, of which in a few years I became one of the most influential members, and I still see it as an excellent "prospectus-index" of the book on Ferenczi that I would have liked to write but have never written. My interest in Ferenczi's thought and clinical experience in fact goes back to the time of my graduation thesis in 1971 to 1972, and it has continued unbroken in the years since then, leading me from 1997 onwards to publish many articles on his specific way of working with patients, translated into numerous languages, and various collections of international writings in his honour.

References

Balint, M. (1968). *The Basic Fault: Therapeutic Aspects of Regression*. London: Tavistock.

Berman, E. (1998). La psychanalyse relationnelle. Un arrière-plan historique. *Le Coq-Héron*, Special Issue "Ferenczi à Madrid": 47–60.

Bion, W. R. (1992). *Cogitations*. London: Karnac.

Bollas, C. (1987). *The Shadow of the Object: Psychoanalysis of the Unthought Known*. London: Free Association Books.

Bollas, C. (1989). *Forces of Destiny: Psychoanalysis and Human Idiom*. London: Free Association Books.

Borgogno, F. (1995). Prefazione all'edizione italiana di E. Rayner, *Gli Indipendenti nella psicoanalisi britannica* [Preface to the Italian edition by E. Rayner, *Independents in British Psychoanalysis*] (pp. ix–xxiv). Milan: Cortina.

Borgogno, F. (1997). Un contributo di Ferenczi alla psicoanalisi infantile: la pensabilità del trauma e del traumatico. *Richard e Piggle, 5*: 3 [A contribution by Ferenczi to child psychoanalysis: the trauma and the traumatic are they thinkable? In: F. Borgogno, 1999a].

Borgogno, F. (1999a). *Psicoanalisi come percorso*. Torino: Bollati Boringhieri [*Psychoanalysis as a Journey*. London: Open Gate Press, 2007].

Borgogno, F. (1999b). Sándor Ferenczi's first paper considered as a "calling card." *International Forum of Psychoanalysis, 8*(3/4): 249–256.

Borgogno, F. (2002). Perché Ferenczi oggi. In: F. Borgogno (a cura di), *Ferenczi oggi*. Bollati Boringhieri, Torino, 2004 [Why Ferenczi today? The contribution of Sándor Ferenczi to the understanding and healing of psychic suffering. *International Forum of Psychoanalysis, 13*: 5–13, 2004].

Borgogno, F. (2006). Ferenczi and Winnicott: searching for a "missing link" (of the soul). *American Journal of Psychoanalysis, 67*: 221–234, 2007.

Borgogno, F. (2007). The relevance of "role reversal" in today's psychoanalytic work. *International Forum of Psychoanalysis, 17*: 213–220, 2008.

Borgogno, F. (2009). Sándor Ferenczi, the "introjective psychoanalyst". *American Imago, 68*(2): 155–172, 2011.

Borgogno, F. (2011). *La signorina che faceva hara-kiri e altri saggi.* Torino: Bollati Boringhieri [*The Girl Who Committed Hara-Kiri and Other Historico-Clinical Essays.* London: Karnac, 2013].

Borgogno, F., & Merciai, S. A. (2000). Searching for Bion. Cogitations: a new *Clinical Diary?* In: P. B. Talamo, F. Borgogno, & S. A. Merciai (Eds.), *W. R. Bion: Between Past and Future* (pp. 56–78). London/New York: Karnac.

Borgogno, F. & Vigna-Taglianti, M. (2012). Role-reversal and the dissociation of the self. Actions signalling memories to be recovered: an exploration of a somewhat neglected transference-countertransference process. In: R. Oelsner (Ed.), *Transference and Countertransference Today.* London: Karnac, 2013.

Faimberg, H. (1996). Listening to listening. *International Journal of Psychoanalysis, 77*(4): 667–677.

Fédida, P. (1992). *Crise et contre-transfert.* Paris: Presses Universitaires de France.

Ferenczi, S. (1908a). The effect on women of premature ejaculation in men. In: *Final Contributions to the Problems and Methods of Psycho-Analysis* (pp. 291–294). London: Karnac.

Ferenczi, S. (1908b). Actual- and psycho-neuroses in the light of Freud's investigations and psycho-analysis. In: *Further Contributions to the Theory and Technique of Psycho-Analysis* (pp. 30–54). London: Karnac.

Ferenczi, S. (1908c). Psycho-analysis and education. In: *Final Contributions to the Problems and Methods of Psycho-Analysis* (pp. 280–290). London: Karnac.

Ferenczi, S. (1909). Introjection and transference. In: *First Contributions to the Theory and Technique of Psycho-Analysis* (pp. 35–93). London: Karnac.

Ferenczi, S. (1912a). On transitory symptom-constructions during the analysis. In: *First Contributions to the Theory and Technique of Psycho-Analysis* (pp. 193–212). London: Karnac.

Ferenczi, S. (1912b). Suggestion and psycho-analysis. In: *Further Contributions to the Theory and Technique of Psycho-Analysis* (pp. 55–67). London: Karnac.

Ferenczi, S. (1913a). Taming of a wild horse. In: *Final Contributions to the Problems and Methods of Psycho-Analysis* (pp. 336–340). London: Karnac.

Ferenczi, S. (1913b). Belief, disbelief and conviction. In: *Further Contributions to the Theory and Technique of Psycho-Analysis* (pp. 437–449). London: Karnac.

Ferenczi, S. (1913c). A transitory symptom: the position during treatment. In: *Further Contributions to the Theory and Technique of Psycho-Analysis* (p. 242). London: Karnac.

Ferenczi, S. (1915). Psychogenic anomalies of voice production. In: *Further Contributions to the Theory and Technique of Psycho-Analysis* (pp. 105–109). London: Karnac.

Ferenczi, S. (1919a). On the technique of psycho-analysis. In: *Further Contributions to the Theory and Technique of Psycho-Analysis* (pp. 177–188). London: Karnac.

Ferenczi, S. (1919b). Thinking and muscle innervation. In: *Further Contributions to the Theory and Technique of Psycho-Analysis* (pp. 230–232). London: Karnac.

Ferenczi, S. (1919c). Technical difficulties in the analysis of a case of hysteria. In: *Further Contributions to the Theory and Technique of Psycho-Analysis* (pp. 189–197). London: Karnac.

Ferenczi, S. (1920–1932). Notes and fragments. In: *Final Contributions to the Problems and Methods of Psycho-Analysis* (pp. 216–279). London: Karnac.

Ferenczi, S. (1921). The further development of the active therapy in psycho-analysis. In: *Further Contributions to the Theory and Technique of Psycho-Analysis* (pp. 198–216). London: Karnac.

Ferenczi, S. (1924a). On forced phantasies. In: *Further Contributions to the Theory and Technique of Psycho-Analysis* (pp. 68–77). London: Karnac.

Ferenczi, S. (1924b). The science which lulls and the science which awakens. *Nyugat*, No 1 [not included in English editions of Ferenczi's works].

Ferenczi, S. (1925). Psycho-analysis of sexual habit. In: *Further Contributions to the Theory and Technique of Psycho-Analysis* (pp. 259–297). London: Karnac.

Ferenczi, S. (1926). A review of Rank's "Technik der Psychoanalyse". *International Journal of Psychoanalysis*, 8: 93–100.

Ferenczi, S. (1927a). The adaptation of the family to the child. In: *Final Contributions to the Problems and Methods of Psycho-Analysis* (pp. 61–76). London: Karnac.

Ferenczi, S. (1927b). The problem of the termination of the analysis. In: *Final Contributions to the Problems and Methods of Psycho-Analysis* (pp. 77–86). London: Karnac.

Ferenczi, S. (1928a). The elasticity of psycho-analytic technique. In: *Final Contributions to the Problems and Methods of Psycho-Analysis* (pp. 87–101). London: Karnac.

Ferenczi, S. (1928b). La preparazione dello psicoanalista [The training of the psychoanalyst]. In: *Opere* (1927–1933), vol 4. Milano: R. Cortina, 2002 [Original edition: *Über den Lehrgang des Psychoanalytikers. Bausteine zur Psychoanalyse, Band III: Arbeiten aus den Jahren 1908–1933*. Bern: Huber, 1964. Not included in English editions of Ferenczi's works].

Ferenczi, S. (1929). The principle of relaxation and neocatharsis. In: *Final Contributions to the Problems and Methods of Psycho-Analysis* (pp. 108–125). London: Karnac.

Ferenczi, S. (1931). Child analysis in the analysis of adults. In: *Final Contributions to the Problems and Methods of Psycho-Analysis* (pp. 126–155). London: Karnac.

Ferenczi, S. (1932a). Confusion of tongues between adults and the child. In: *Final Contributions to the Problems and Methods of Psycho-Analysis* (pp. 156–167). London: Karnac.

Ferenczi, S. (1932b). *The Clinical Diary*, J. Dupont (Ed.). Cambridge, MA: Harvard University Press.

Ferenczi, S., & Rank, O. (1924). *The Development of Psycho-Analysis*. Madison, CT: International Universities Press, 1986.

Ferro, A. (1992). *The Bi-personal Field*. London/New York: Routledge, 1999.

Freud, S. (1904). On psychotherapy. *S. E., 7*: 255–268. London: Hogarth.

Freud, S. (1906). Psycho-analysis and the establishment of the facts in legal proceedings. *S. E., 9*: 97–114. London: Hogarth.

Freud, S. (1908). On the sexual theories of children. *S. E., 9*: 205–226. London: Hogarth.

Freud, S. (1909). *Analysis of a Phobia in a Five-Year-Old Boy. S. E., 10*: 1–150. London: Hogarth.

Freud, S. (1912). Recommendations to physicians practising psycho-analysis. *S. E., 12*: 109–120. London: Hogarth.

Freud, S., & Ferenczi, S. (1908–1933). *The Correspondence of Sigmund Freud and Sándor Ferenczi (1908–1933)*. Volume I: 1908–1914, E. Brabant, E. Falzeder, & P. Giampieri-Deutsch (Eds.). Cambridge, MA: Harvard University Press, 1993; Volume II: 1914–1919, E. Falzeder & E. Brabant (Eds.). Cambridge, MA: Harvard University Press, 1996; Volume III: 1920–1933, E. Falzeder & E. Brabant (Eds.). Cambridge, MA: Harvard University Press, 2000.

Granoff, W. (1958). Ferenczi: faux problème ou vrai malentendu? [Ferenczi: false problem or true misunderstanding?] In: W. Granoff (Ed.), *Lacan, Ferenczi and Freud*. Paris: Gallimard, 2001.

Haynal, A. (2001). *Disappearing and Reviving: Sándor Ferenczi in the History of Psychoanalysis*. London: Karnac, 2002.

Heimann, P. (1989). *About Children and Children-no-longer. Collected Papers 1942–1980*, M. Tonnesmann (Ed.). London: Routledge and the Institute of Psycho-Analysis.

Jacobs, T. (1986). On countertransference enactments. *Journal of American Psychoanalytic Association*, 34(2): 289–307.

Klein, M. (1946). Notes on some schizoid mechanisms. *International Journal of Psychoanalysis*, 27: 99–110

Lorin, C., & Almassy, K. (1983). Ferenczi, traducteur-interpretant [Ferenczi, translator–interpreter]. *Perspectives Psychiatriques*, 3: 92.

Mészáros, J. (Ed.) (1999). *Ferenczi Sándor: A pszichoanalízis felé. Fiatalkori írások: 1897–1908*. Budapest: Osiris Könyvkiadó [*Sándor Ferenczi: Toward Psychoanalysis. Early Works: 1897–1908*].

Ogden, T. H. (2001). *Conversations at the Frontier of Dreaming*. Northvale, NJ: Jason Aronson

Rosenfeld, H. (1987). *Impasse and Interpretation*. London: Tavistock.

CHAPTER 11

Ferenzci's ideas in contemporary psychoanalysis: Ferenczi's contribution to the psychoanalytic theory of trauma and further developments

Luis J. Martín Cabré

Introduction by Maria José Gonçalves

Luis Martín Cabré, psychoanalyst, full member with didactic functions, and past president of the Psychoanalytical Association of Madrid, is a profound connoisseur of the work of Sándor Ferenczi, as well as the author of *Authenticity and Reciprocity. A Dialogue with Ferenczi*.

A co-founding member of the Sándor Ferenczi International Foundation and the Sándor Ferenczi International Study Group of Madrid, he has contributed to the development of Ferenczian thought in the light of contemporary psychoanalysis.

The theoretical and clinical thought of the father of object relationship theories, for some years in the shadows, has become unavoidable and has been the subject of numerous initiatives, one of the most recent being the installation, in 2011, of an archives centre—the Ferenczi House in Budapest—acquired by the Sándor Ferenczi Foundation as its headquarters, library, and scientific meeting place.

Thanks to the Iberian psychoanalysis meetings which have been held regularly since 2009 and which promote scientific and personal exchanges amongst the members of the three Iberian societies of psychoanalysis, Luis Cabré has become a regular visitor to Lisbon, where he has developed solid friendships and has made an invaluable scientific contribution, particularly in the renewed interest of Portuguese psychoanalysts in Ferenczi's work.

Currently, Ferenczi is an author whose texts are part of the regular training of Portuguese Psychoanalytical Society candidates and several scientific events have been held around Ferenczi's thought.

For Ferenczi, it is the primary object which, by its action, determines the destiny of the drive and the future psychic organisation of the individual. As such, the trauma reflects the result of the failure of maternal empathy and the disruption of primary care. It is in his seminal article "Confusion of languages" that he defines his concept of trauma and provides a long description of the psychic mechanisms that allow the ego of the subject to survive the death of a part of the self.

In this text, Luis Cabré presents Ferenczi's ideas on trauma, namely regarding the unrepresentability of early traumatic experiences, in the psyche. The unrepresentability of trauma refers to a timeless state of non-transformation and desymbolisation, which Winnicott would later develop theoretically and technically when he introduced the concept of the false self.

The author also points out that, for Ferenczi, since trauma is a phenomenon located in the objectal area, it necessarily alters the relations with both the external object and the representation of internal objects, a theory which Klein adopted and developed.

Luis Cabré, in a contemporary approach to trauma, asks himself, and us, whether extreme behaviours of violence or self-destruction conceal devastating and cumulative experiences in the unconscious, unable to be represented, and whether psychoanalytic listening can turn them into an experience of humanisation.

* * *

In many of today's psychoanalytic theorisations, which build upon Ferenczi's contributions about the theory and the clinical aspects of the traumatic theory, the notion of trauma is shown as an invasion—of passion, love, folly, or hatred towards some other, into the subject's ego.

Ferenczi developed his theory on trauma starting from his clinical experience with borderline cases, and he presented it in his last texts, especially in his famous work on "Confusion of tongues between the adults and the child", where he would attribute a determinant role to the external objects in the structuration of the child's psychic apparatus, and he would underscore two essential arguments for the psychoanalytical theory: the identification processes and the splitting of the ego. By extending the seduction concept that had been theorised by Freud, Ferenczi made a considerable theoretical advance, as he presented the traumatic aetiology as the result of a *psychic violation* of a child by an adult, a *confusion of tongues* between them, and above all a *disavowal* (*Verleugnung*) on the part of the adult over the child's despair.

Splitting and autotomy

When the passion language of an adult, who unconsciously manoeuvres the eroticism of both love and hate, clashes violently with the language of tenderness of the child, disowning and disavowing the acknowledgement in the psychic apparatus of the child—who had deposited all his/her trust in the adult—of those thinking and affects, a trauma takes place that provokes not only fear, disappointment, and pain but, and above all else, inevitably leads to a splitting. In contrast with the splitting in Freud, according to which a part of the ego accepts the reality while other disavows it, in Ferenczi's conception a part dies and the other lives on, but devoid of affects, remaining excluded from its own existence as if it is someone else who is living its life. In addition to splitting, infantile trauma may generate fragmentation, atomisation, and autotomy. We would underscore this last notion of autotomy coined by him, which implies the amputation of a part of oneself, so from a Ferenczian perspective a part of the subject "dies" through splitting. It does not feel pain because it does not exist any more. Even further:

> he is no longer worried about breathing or about the preservation of his life in general. Moreover, he regards being destroyed or mutilated with interest, as if it is no longer his own self but another person who is undergoing these torments. (Ferenczi, 1932, p. 6)

The psyche defends itself by means of its self-destruction, or else by destroying whomever offers help or affect.

Therefore, the concept of trauma, and above all the idea of psychic commotion that would be described years later by Ferenczi in *The Clinical Diary*, refers to an unstoppable *breakdown* (collapse/downfall) and to a loss of one's identity, with the consequent submission and unconditional docility produced by the traumatic experience, which destroys the ability of the ego to psychically elaborate it, as is the case in the fascinating clinical description he makes of his patient O.S.[1] There we read about the loss of the sense of time, "as though life did not have to come to an end in old age and death" (Ferenczi, 1932, p. 142). Now, this is not a defence mechanism, but a survival one. Paradoxically, this extreme answer arises for the purpose of saving one's life. In order to safeguard one's spirit and integrity it is necessary to sacrifice the live portion of the body and submit oneself to a self-treatment, to an autotomy in which the person has to abstract from oneself and from the others. Would this not make us think in psychosis?

However, in a previous work, "On the revision of the interpretation of dreams" (1931), Ferenczi had already discovered that the splits of the ego caused by early traumatic experiences were defence mechanisms that preceded the establishment of repression. As Ferenczi said, "no memory traces of such impressions remain, even in the unconscious" (Ferenczi, 1931, p. 240).

As a consequence, in his theoretical concept—later developed by him with greater precision—trauma becomes transformed into something that is not represented in the psyche. The reaction to pain belongs to the order of the non-representable and is inaccessible to memory and recall. From this point of view, to Ferenczi the trauma "presents" itself, instead of being "re-presented": its presence does not belong to any present time, and even destroys the present in which it seems to introduce itself. It is, then, a present without presence, a crazy present, in which the subject gets out of the time while trying to place his/her unthinkable suffering into a greater temporal unit, out of any mere everydayness or historical temporality. This is an infinite and inexhaustible present, but at the same time it is completely void.

---

[1] *The Clinical Diary*, 26 June 1932 (1932, pp. 140–143).

Hence, Ferenczi places his theory of the trauma in the dimension of a "present" that stays outside of the historical temporality. Unlike in the historical present, which settles a presence and an identity, in this traumatic present everything becomes dissolved: there is no subject, nor opposition between subject and object. What Ferenczi suggests to us is that, in this dynamics and time of the trauma, something is hinted at that has to do with death, and cannot be represented. To Ferenczi, such is in fact "… a process of dissolution that moves toward total dissolution, that is to say, death" (Ferenczi, 1932, p. 130). But, perhaps, more than to a death that sets a limit, what Ferenczi refers to is to indefinitely dying, in a time in which nothing commences. Time gets mummified and, acting as a death tissue, prevents and paralyses the function of the *après coup*.

But confronted with the impossibility of being represented, the body becomes the only addressee of the traumatic memory. That memory, bound to stay inside the body, enslaves the latter in the role of a spokesperson and transforms it into a martyr of the word that has lost its voice. The only chance of relief for this body lies in rebuilding the trauma and placing it back in the intersubjective space of the transference/countertransference of the psychoanalytic relationship. But how? By means of what therapeutic instrument?

Subsequent developments

After Ferenczi's death, his "scandalous" ideas about trauma, as well as the technical innovations derived from them, seemed to vanish from psychoanalytic theorisations. However, like the effect of a silent transmission, several of his most brilliant intuitions eventually managed to come back, were reconsidered from quite divergent theoretical formulations, and opened new paths in psychoanalysis.

Whilst for Freud the trauma as a consequence of a sexual seduction had been the key factor in the aetiology of neurosis, for Ferenczi it was the expression of a disorder in the communication between the child and the adult, that is to say, a *"confusion of tongues"*. This linguistic dimension would offer a point of contact with some of Lacan's conceptions, for whom the trauma would be close to his conception of *"the real"*, would resist symbolisation and language, and consequently would be unassimilable. If we configure the Oedipus complex as the ultimate expression of the symbolic order, the sexual incest that Ferenczi was referring to could only be understood as a breakdown of such order and as a *"confusion"* among the registers of the Real, the Symbolic and the Imaginary, that is, among an unassimilable experience, the truth, and the fantasy.

For Ferenczi, trauma places itself in the context of the relationship. Unlike in the Freudian conception, where trauma determines the destiny of the drives, in Ferenczi the trauma modifies the object relations, both with the external object and with their internal representations. Klein's (1935) conception of the good object as a container for the expression of the child's needs seems to be related to the ideas of her first analyst.[2] If, for Klein, the trauma is defined in relation with the frustration of internal impulses and the projection of rage over the bad objects and the subsequent defensive introjection, their followers, the so-called post-Kleinians, would not fail to underscore the important role of the frustrating real experiences as agents for the intensity of the child's destructive desires.

Ferenczi brought to the table the discussion about the constitutional nature of pulsions. His thesis on the exogenesis of the neurosis became the first draft of a psychoanalytic psychology and of a theory of object relations. Outstanding authors in the theory of object relations, such as Fairbairn or Guntrip, adhere almost unilaterally to Ferenczi's conceptions of such. This theory contributed to a progressive broadening of the trauma concept. Traumatic situations arise from inadequate caring on the part of primary objects. Many analysts, Bowlby amongst them, attribute the disorders in the emotional development of the child to the inadequacy of the early maternal care. Mahler's assertion that the actual behaviour of the primary object was of significance has a similar meaning.

Building upon Ferenczi's observations and incorporating some of the ideas of Freud to the theory of object relations, Balint (1969) proposed a three-stage theory of trauma, emphasising again the effect of disavowal on its genesis. But, perhaps the author who most faithfully recovered the intuitions of Ferenczi was Winnicott. Among his most significant

---

[2] Melanie Klein underwent an analysis of several years with Ferenczi. Once settled in Berlin, she would undertake a second analysis with Abraham that would be dramatically interrupted by the unexpected death of the latter.

theoretical contributions, we have his extension of the concept of trauma and his conception of *relative trauma* (1953) as a consequence of a *not good-enough mother* regarding the functions required by the child. Leaning on these observations, Khan (1963) coined the concept of *cumulative trauma* highlighting the effects exerted on the child by the fractures in the para-excitation function of the mother. This extended perspective on trauma would also include: the distinction introduced by Kris (1956) between *shock trauma* and *strain trauma*;[3] Greenacre's (1952) thesis about *screen memories* that conceal traumas; Waelder's (1967) idea of "constructive traumas" in psychological development;[4] Sandler's (1967) "retrospective trauma"; Ekstein's (1963) conceptualisation on the difference between *positive* and *negative* trauma; as well as Baranger et al's (1987) distinction between *pure trauma* and historicisation. Drawing from Winnicott, Green (1982, 1986) stresses the *negative hallucination of the mother* and proposes the concept of the *dead mother* as a screen for an irrepresentable void.

Ferenczi set up, too, the fundamentals of a psychology of early disorders, and discovered the primitive defence mechanisms, unknown until then, especially the splitting processes, which psychological consequences would be developed years later by Winnicott in his theorisation on the concept of *false self*. Whilst Bion does not try to study the effects of trauma, but the psychotic thinking, he describes the splitting and fragmentation mechanisms that allude to self-destructive processes of the ego, or parts of it, and to their eviction from the psychical apparatus. Several paragraphs of his works on the development of schizophrenic thinking (Bion, 1956) and on the differentiation between the psychotic

---

[3] Thus it seems that we are not always and only rarely with the desirable sharpness able to distinguish between the effects of two kinds of traumatic situations; between the effect of a single experience, when reality powerfully and often suddenly impinges on the child's life—the shock trauma as I should like to call it—and the effect of long-lasting situations, which may cause traumatic effects by the accumulation of frustrating tensions—the strain trauma as I would like to say. (Kris, 1956, p. 54)

[4] Building upon the ideas of Greenacre (1967) about the dangers of traumas in the pre-oedipal stage, Waelder highlights how the mechanism of transformation from passivity (stuporous reactions) into activity (shouting, reacting, or escaping) is an index for a better resolution of the traumatic impact.

and non-psychotic parts of the personality (Bion, 1957) are evocative of some of Ferenczi's descriptions in *The Clinical Diary*.

Challenges in contemporary clinical practice

If the traumas of a sexual nature which prevent the development of the ability for enjoyment pave the way to sexual inhibitions, frigidity, and above all the phantasies and the sadomasochistic pleasure, the traumas of a non-sexual nature tear apart the sense of confidence in the world and the transitional space that enables the feeling of being in harmony with others, of being the bearer of desires, and of projecting oneself on life through an internal world dense with thoughts and emotions. When a child feels as having been systematically disavowed and neglected in his thoughts and qualities, his/her emotional and affective world resented in its entirety. The child has now to reconcile his/her expectant yearning for good-enough parents with the disavowed reality of not having found appreciation for his/her love. Around a child that has been wounded and deprived of a shared emotional world, an apparently normal adolescent may become structured, but behind it a person will be hidden who will not have available a free and confident emotional field, and in whom the unelaborated traumatic experience destroys the possibility of perceiving oneself as a whole person. And here we have the starting point for a possibly perverse or psychotic structure, or dynamics.

We are still far from having reached a unification and integration of all the parameters that remain opened in the psychoanalytic theory, starting with the challenge posed by the clinical experience with traumatised patients who develop attitudes, mechanisms, and an organisation of emotions and feelings of a perverse, psychopathic, or psychotic nature. However, when hearing patients who practise sadomasochistic relationships, or certain compulsive situations of physical self-harm through supposedly aesthetic surgery interventions, with issues of anorexia/bulimia, or the unexplored issue of incest, either practised by fathers or mothers, problems of physical abuses and humiliation of women or children, the unwarranted cruelty on persons in a weak or submissive position, torture in all its aberrant forms of application, racism and xenophobia, war, hatred, and ultimately, perhaps, when confronted with a world that seemingly is not willing to renounce to a single drive, it leads us to wonder ourselves as psychoanalysts about what devastating experiences have become accumulated in that non-repressed unconscious to which I referred earlier, which are responsible for so much violence and destruction.

Perhaps the hearing and the reflection on the relationship between trauma and other pathologies may allow us to think that psychoanalysis will always have the opportunity to exist and to stand as an alternative to quick and superficial therapies or pharmacological treatments because, as Piera Aulagnier said, most of the time the patients do not come to our sessions looking for an intellectual value or the deciphering of a truth, they come simply because they need to count on the help of a human presence, able to understand their pain, but above all able to enable them to keep on living.

References

Balint, M. (1969). Trauma and object relationship. *International Journal of Psychoanalysis, 50*(4): 429–435.

Baranger, M., Baranger, W., & Mom, J. (1987). El Trauma psíquico infantil, de nosotros a Freud. Trauma puro, retroactividad y reconstrucción [Childhood psychic trauma, from us to Freud. Pure trauma, retroactivity and reconstruction]. *Revista de Psicoanálisis, 44*(4), Buenos Aires.

Bion, W. R. (1956). Development of schizophrenic thought. In: *Second Thoughts: Selected Papers on Psychoanalysis* (pp. 36–42). London: Heinemann, 1967.

Bion, W. R. (1957). Differentiation of the psychotic from the non-psychotic personalities. In: *Second Thoughts: Selected Papers on Psychoanalysis* (pp. 43–64). London: Heinemann, 1967.

Ekstein, R. (1963). Pleasure and reality, play and work, thought and action—variations of and on a theme. *Journal of Humanistic Psychology, 3*(2): 20–31.

Ferenczi, S. (1931). On the revision of the interpretation of dreams. In: M. Balint (Ed.), *Final Contributions to the Problems and Methods of Psycho-Analysis.* New York: Basic Books, 1955.

Ferenczi, S. (1932). *The Clinical Diary of Sándor Ferenczi*, J. Dupont (Ed.). Cambridge, MA: Harvard University Press, 1988 [French edition, 1985, Paris: Payot].

Green, A. (1982). *Narcissisme de vie, narcissisme de mort* [*Narcissism of life, narcissism of death*]. Paris: Minuit.

Green, A. (1986). Le travail du négatif [The work of the negative]. *Revue française de psychanalyse*, *L*(1): 489–493.

Greenacre, P. (Ed.) (1952). *Trauma, Growth and Personality*. New York: W. W. Norton.

Greenacre, P. (1967). The influence of infantile trauma in genetic patterns. In: S. S. Furst (Ed.), *Psychic Trauma* (pp. 108–153). New York: Basic Books.

Khan, M. M. R. (1963). The concept of cumulative trauma. In: *The Privacy of the Self* (pp. 42–58). London: Hogarth, 1974.

Klein, M. (1935). A contribution to the psychogenesis of manic-depressive states. *The International Journal of Psychoanalysis*, *16*: 145–174.

Kris, E. (1956). The recovery of childhood memories in psychoanalysis. *Psychoanalytic Study of the Child*, *11*: 54–88.

Sandler, J. (1967). Trauma, strain and development. In: S. S. Furst (Ed.), *Psychic Trauma* (pp. 154–174). New York: Basic Books.

Waelder, R. (1967). Trauma and the variety of extraordinary challenges. In: S. S. Furst (Ed.), *Psychic Trauma* (pp. 221–234). New York: Basic Books.

Winnicott, D. W. (1953). Psychoses and child care. *British Journal of Medical Psychology*, *26*: 68–74.

Final thoughts

In Portugal, the second decade of the twenty-first century has been intense and demanding in psychoanalysis. Under unfavourable economic, social, and scientific conditions, the opportunity to transform, develop, and create, rather than just learning, was absolutely crucial.

The dialogue with other thinkers and the effort of attentive listening were essential skills, sometimes difficult to understand and tolerate within us, that provided change and enhanced growth.

The compilation of texts organised in this volume aims to leave a "print" testimony of an accomplished and hopeful experience which the editors leave for future generations of psychoanalysts, mental health professionals, and restless souls. It is the result of taking, for a moment, a privileged position to put into perspective the scope of multiple actions and efforts, combining exchange of experiences and genuine mobilisation of the will to learn and improve, that is not always immediate or entirely conscious.

In these chapters we consider that the authors offered very significant contributions to position psychoanalysis and psychoanalytical culture today in an unrivalled place, in what it reaches, and stands for: contemporary and attuned to the transformation brought forwards by technological developments (as illustrated by Andrea Marzi); their conceptual implications, but also to clinical practice (read the key chapters by Howard Levine and David Bell); able to integrate history and recover major authors as, for instance, the return to the reflection on the contributions of Ferenczi, whose relevance is justified by its importance in the development of the object relation theories and the concept of intersubjectivity in the analytical cure (with two brilliant participations from Franco Borgogno and Luis Martín Cabré); mark the presence of the unconscious at the core of the body and sexuality (with Fernando Orduz); and in culture and social politics (exceptional works from Virginia Ungar, Leopold Nosek and Éric Smadja); and lastly, the history of psychoanalysis and psychoanalytical institutions (two keys chapters, both published here for the first time by Robert Hinshelwood and Sergio Eduardo Nick).

The originality and timeliness of the authors' thoughts, whose generosity in sharing for which we are very grateful, finds a match in the honour and genuine way in which we feel and welcome them.

We are certain that the Lisbon Lectures transformed many of the colleagues who attended the meeting. We believe that they can also spark enthusiasm in all of those who access them now through this book.

Index